Pioneer Mother on the River of No Return:
The Life of Isabella Kelly Benedict Robie

Pioneer Mother on the River of No Return:

The Life of Isabella Kelly Benedict Robie

by

Herman Wiley Ronnenberg

𝓗𝓦𝓡

Heritage Witness Reflections Publishing

517 South Elm

P.O. Box 356

Troy, Idaho 83871-0356

Pioneer Mother on the River of No Return:
The Life of Isabella Kelly Benedict Robie
by Herman Wiley Ronnenberg

HWR

Heritage Witness Reflections Publishing
P.O. Box 356
Troy, Idaho 83871-0356

Cover painting of Isabella by Liz Hess

Book and cover design
LongfeatherBookDesign.com

Indexing by Debbie Olson
Proof reading by Kim Farbo
Editing by Celia Flinn

ISBN: 978-0-9818408-4-0 (paperback)
ISBN: 978-0-9910891-1-6 (ebook)
LCCN: 2012916996

*This book is dedicated to all the descendants,
and all the relatives of Isabella, and especially to
Deb Starr, whose research made this book possible.*

Contents

Illustration Numbers and Page Numbers

LIFE AT FREEDOM & WHITE BIRD

START OF THE NEZ PERCE WAR

MARY CAROLINE'S DIARY

AFTER 1879

Introduction

My interest in Isabella's life story began as an offshoot of my research on her close friend, Jeanette Manuel. Jeanette's husband, John J. (Jack) Manuel, was the owner of the brewery in Warren, Idaho. He was included in the research completed of the lives and businesses of all of Idaho's brewers. Finding the acorn of Isabella's story, so to speak, involved a convoluted trail from the trunk of the oak. In October of 2009, I published a brief synopsis of Isabella's life story in *Echoes of the Past*, the journal published by the Historical Museum at St. Gertrude's Monastery near Cottonwood, Idaho. Shortly after, Deborah Starr of Orofino, Idaho, contacted me to say she was a great granddaughter of Isabella and had a great deal of research material to share.

Deborah's long painstaking research made this book possible. Everyone interested in Idaho history owes her a debt of gratitude. Over the years she had gathered a large hoard of documents, family memories, and photos. The historian's task is light when the documents are all assembled. Mike Peterson of Grangeville, another relative of Isabella and a history buff, also read and commented on the manuscript and provided an additional photo. Mrs. Lillian Heytvelt of Pomeroy, Washington, read, corrected, and commented on the manuscript. Celia Flinn edited the manuscript next. Though my interest in Isabella's story took a while to develop, I find her as fascinating as any Idaho pioneer.

Isabella shared 15 years of her life with her friend Jeanette. They were the co-belles of the ball in Florence, Idaho, at the dance celebrating the new year 1863. In June of 1877, Isabella was the last woman to see Jeanette alive. Isabella, however, had a long life ahead when the Nez Perce War ended that autumn. Isabella had five children with Samuel Benedict, and four more with her second husband, Edward Robie. Her descendants made enormous contributions to Idaho and the Northwest in the last century and a half. Isabella's story helps us remember the sacrifices and the values that enabled the first generation of Idaho pioneers to stay and build a new culture. Above all though, it is a marvelous human adventure story.

The diary kept by Isabella's daughter, Mary Caroline, "Caddie," or "Carrie," while they owned the boarding house in Grangeville, is a document of great value. It provides an understanding of the lives and the comings and goings of the people of that region during 1878 and the way they were perceived by a young girl. It may be challenging to read but it is worth the effort. There was not yet a local newspaper, and this diary may be the only record of life at that time and place.

Isabella lived in a world in which gunfights, vigilantes, lynchings, and military actions against native peoples were all a threat to the innocent and guilty alike. There were also family-sized conflicts involving choice of marriage partners, religion, generational conflict, and alcohol abuse. Isabella observed as much in one lifetime as anyone could, despite spending her adult life all in one county of one western state.

The Salmon River of Idaho is the longest river in the lower 48 states that both starts and ends within a single state. It is, and was alternately known, as the River of No Return, as its swift current made upstream travel next to impossible. This exciting alternate name has been used as a punch line, a movie title and in several books. "No Return" could be a metaphor for Isabella's life, as each episode went into entirely new territory, making the return to previous homes and situations next to impossible. Isabella's life truly shows how pivotal

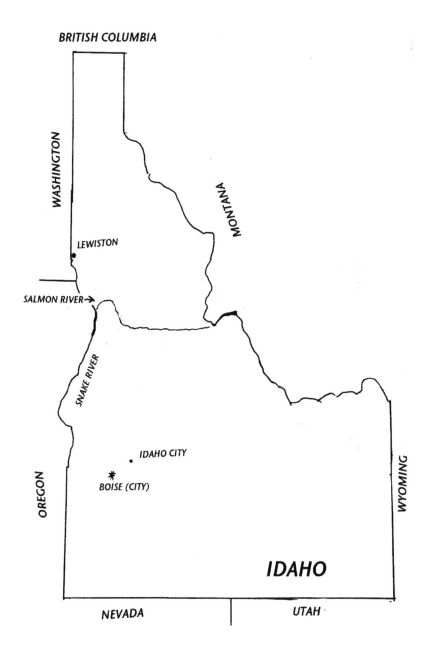

events, such as gold rushes and Indian wars, impact individuals and families. Likewise, it depicts how individuals influence the larger stage that is our collective history.

1

THE RESCUE

June-December 1877

HOLDING HER THREE YEAR-OLD DAUGHTER, Addie, in her arms and clinging to the hand of eight-year-old Frances, Isabella said goodbye to her old friend Jeanette Manuel, and began the steep 12-mile climb out of White Bird Canyon to Mount Idaho. Her husband was dead. Her friends were comforting but of little assistance, and her children were already getting sick from hunger, exertion and fear. Menacing hostiles—perhaps the same men who killed her husband—were potentially everywhere and the road was not safe. With only her motherly instincts and Irish determination to strengthen her, Isabella summoned her courage and plowed ahead.

Isabella's son, Grant, and daughter, Mary Caroline, were already at Mount Idaho where they had been boarding so they could study during the school term. The body of precocious little Nettie, her fifth child, had been safe under the sod of Idaho for nearly four years. All of Isabella's attention was on the two girls that clung to her.

Isabella later recalled conditions at the Manuel ranch that she was then leaving: "The Indians had eaten every morsel in the house before they left and I could not even get a crust at Mrs. Manuel's."[1] The arduous hike would be without nourishment.

On that Friday night, as Frances remembered it, the family continued on their way toward Mount Idaho staying close to the road while fearing to venture completely on to it and become visible at any distance.[2] Soon after starting their journey, a horseman came by on the run and shots rang out. The rider was settler William George, and he made good his escape.

A report written years later recalled that: "While on this terrible journey she discovered a white man, mounted upon a swift strong horse flying for his life. She hailed him and begged him to help her. Oh, shame! He refused. This is the solitary act recorded of an Idahoan in those trying times of war for which all brave men blush. The mother begged him to take her youngest babe and save it. He refused. This man still lives and his home is on Camas Prairie. This unchivalrous man reported in Mount Idaho that Mrs. Benedict was probably killed by the Indians; and if not, she was a wanderer on the mountain."[3] This may or may not be a memory of this particular encounter. Such a happening had to further try Isabella's resolve and increase her fear. Fear, desperation, and hunger were the unseen baggage Isabella lugged alongside her children on this journey.

Frances recalled: "Knowing there were Indians in the vicinity we were loathe to venture forth, but Mother, brave little soul, knew she had to battle along and, undaunted, pushed on, avoiding the road as much as possible."[4] As the three Benedicts forged ahead, they heard a bear at a spring near the Theodore Swarts place. Frances, the future Mrs. Shissler, held tight to her mother's skirt and warned, "A bear is in our way and we can't pass." Isabella told her child she was not afraid of the bear but was afraid of the Indians. After an exhausting all-night ordeal, Isabella reached the top of the canyon near the old White Bird Hill Grade where the little family hid in the brush. "When near the top of the mountain Mother told me to sit down and hold the baby, and not move from there, while she climbed to the top to locate the road and reconnoiter before going on. Coming back she called softly, fearing she might miss us in the dark."[5]

Figure 1.1 White Bird Grade sign. Isabella, Frances and Addie walked this steep grade from the Salmon River to the Camas Prairie, June 15-17, 1877. This was about 17 miles. Photo by the author.

"After a short rest she re-traced her steps up the mountain, carrying the baby. With my hand in hers we went over the top and gained the shelter of the brush beside the road. This was the old grade on the White Bird hill." They stayed the rest of Friday night there and moved to deeper brush when the sun came

Figure 1.2 View of White Bird Grade looking north from White Bird Creek. This is the general direction Isabella and her children would have been walking. Photo by the author.

up. Frances carried water to them from a creek using the baby's shoe for a container.[6] "All day Saturday we remained hidden in the brush

Figure 1.3 White Bird Battlefield Kiosk on Hwy 95. The entire battlefield and old trails up the grade can be seen from this spot. Photo by the author.

while the whole tribe of Indians was passing by. They were hurrying their families from their camping ground at the lake, now Tolo Lake, to the Salmon River, aiming to cross before the soldiers came up with them."[7] Saturday, a day of hunger and fear, passed. Dusk at last came on that long June day.

At the Top of White Bird Grade-Isabella squeezed Frances hand even tighter while pushing her other little babe, Addie, lower in the weeds as the sounds of the horses grew ever closer. It was well after midnight and the beginning of June 17. She had concealed her little family from the sight of mounted men several times in the past three days, and knew how to do this well. She heard a muffled bit of speech. It was English, not Nez Perce. She allowed her hopes to lift a bit. Then she heard more horses, and more men despite their attempts to be perfectly quiet. The newly widowed mother of four living children raised her head a bit and peered into the dark of the pre-dawn countryside. It was the cavalry from Fort Lapwai. She nearly collapsed with relief. She picked up Addie and pulled eight—year—old Frances along as they left the brushy hillside and walked toward the men and horses.

The troopers were as surprised to see Isabella as she was to see them. At last she and the children had some food—army hardtack. Soon, Mrs. Isabella Benedict was talking to Captain Perry, the commanding

Figure. 1.4 Battlefield Map. This shows the general flow of the White Bird Battle. Photo by the author.

officer. Her pent-up emotions all gushed forth at once. She was almost too upset to make a coherent story but managed to get out the overall picture. She told him of the attack on the Benedict store, their home, the shooting of her husband, the attack on the Manuel family, and her attempt to take her children to safety at Mount Idaho. Perry told her to spend the rest of the night there and see what the dawn would bring. He ordered one man to give her a blanket and trumpeter Jones gave her his lunch. Knowing a battle was very possible, Perry could spare no men or horses to help her on to Mount Idaho. He offered instead, to send her toward the town with some friendly Nez Perce. Isabella declined.

Figure. 1.5 White Bird Battle site. A closer view of the area. Photo by the author

In General O. O. Howard's report, filed later from second-hand information, he said: Isabella was "burdened with her little ones, and still more heavily with grief at her husband's death, shivering with exposure, hastening, as best she could, to a settlement, the nearest being at least twelve miles distant."

The troopers were in their second night without sleep. They were ordered to make no fires—not even smoking—and to stay awake. One man forgot himself and struck a match to light his pipe.

Figure. 1.6 The north edge of the Battlefield. The view from the top tends to flatten the terrain. It is extremely steep. Photo by the author.

A coyote howl went up immediately and the officers believed their presence had been detected by the Nez Perce Sentries.[8] Most likely, the iron-shod horses had alerted any sentry in the area long before the match was struck. Such a large group had no hope of remaining undetected.

Isabella lay down with her two babes and covered them with the army-issued wool blanket. Physical exhaustion, grief and relief vied for control of her mind. Her children snuggled in close and she slipped into a fitful sleep. Dawn comes early to northern Idaho in June.

Sunday 17 June 1877

At daybreak, Sunday, June 17, Isabella awoke to the sound of the troopers. Sergeant John P. Schorr wrote to historian McWhorter years later that the Benedicts were found in rags and starving.[9] She begged the soldiers not to go further or they would all be massacred. They should have listened.

Perry decided on action. He sent Lieutenant Theller with eight men, including trumpeter Jones, as an advance guard.[10] Within two miles, they were descending down the extremely precipitous White Bird Canyon toward the River of No Return. As they neared the camp close to the Manuel ranch, two Nez Perce scouts with the army told

Theller that six Nez Perce men were approaching from the West as a peace delegation. Without hesitation, Arthur "Ad" Chapman, one of the local civilians with the army, opened fire on the delegation. The war no one wanted had begun. Soon the trumpeter was knocked from his saddle by an amazing shot, eliminating the officers' ability to issue audible commands. The main body of troops saw what had happened and hurried to close ranks with the advance party. The trumpeter with this main body of troops had likewise lost his horn and there was no way to issue commands from the main body of cavalry either.

The volunteers were soon pushed from their position and the soldiers on both flanks believed they had been ordered to retreat. Panic ensued. The officers tried to form a line at several points but without success. The troopers retreat sent them to ever higher ground. That strategic ad-

Figure. 1.7 Center of the battlefield. Photo by the author.

Figure. 1.8 South edge of the battle field. The village of White Bird would be on the right edge, just out of view. U. S. Hwy 95 is on the far right. Photo by the author.

Figure. 1.9 Camas Prairie historical sign. This sign sits near the area the trail taken by Isabella would have first reached the prairie area. Photo by the author.

vantage, and the fact that so many Nez Perce had drunk themselves into a stupor the night before, saved the troopers from a complete annihilation and a repeat of Custer's Last Stand. Any panic-stricken cavalryman still able to travel, went hell bent toward Mount Idaho. Command and control was routed as surely as the men themselves.

Frances Benedict, who was eight years old at the time, remembered that the soldiers who were not killed in the battle retreated in a mad rush to safety and forgot all about the Benedict family. "Had it not been for Charles Crooks, a friend who had joined the local volunteers, we would have been left to the mercy of the Indians. As he reached our hiding place, he halted and said: 'My God, men, you are not going to leave this woman and her children here to be killed are you?'"[11] One account said Charley Crooks halted by Mrs. Benedict, drew his 44 caliber Winchester and told the brigade to pick up the women and children or he'd drop anyone who went past them. Isabella was assisted on to a horse by Mr. Schorr.[12]

Schorr forgot to hand Isabella the bridle reins, according to one account, and Frances remembered her mother had trouble controlling the cavalry mount. Frances was put on behind a soldier and the baby was wrapped in her mother's petticoat and handed to another soldier, "who later dropped her in the road, where she was found and picked up by a volunteer, William Coran (sic)."[13] Billy Coram was the soldier who put Addie over his shoulder, confined in her mother's shawl or petticoat. He arrived at Mount Idaho with the petticoat, but no baby. However, most sources agree that he was the one who did bring the child to safety. Frances, too, fell off. Thus the Benedicts all fell off, were soon afoot, and separated from the soldiers

Figure. 1.10 Close-up of the Camas historical sign. The Camas Prairie is a high-altitude, high-production farming area today. Photo by the author.

Figure. 1.11 Painting by Jo Profers, 1977.
Depicts Wounded Head releasing Isabella to safety.

who had made this half-hearted attempt to help them. The older daughter, Frances, was later picked up and seated on a horse with John Barber, and they reached Mount Idaho safely. "I was later given to Johnny Berger," she recalled.[14] The children, as with all the Salmon River refugees, were taken care of at Loyal Brown's Hotel. At Mount Idaho Mrs. Aram fed Addie drops of milk.[15] Brother, Grant Benedict, was there to meet them, and Frances told him she had seen her mother get on a horse. As the hours dragged on, Isabella did not arrive at Mount Idaho. Ed Robie, who had boarded with the Benedict family the previous winter, questioned Frances about her mother's location when she last saw her.

As it turned out, Isabella had ridden with the main group of terrorized troopers retreating from the battle, but became separated from her children near the Jarrett ranch where her saddle turned and she fell off, and was left afoot again. She tried to find shelter near a spring in the brush when three volunteers came by. She begged them to take her with them. They refused, pleading that their horses were spent and two of the men were wounded. They promised to send help back. Isabella started across the Camas Prairie on foot. She was making good progress when she heard voices and suddenly found herself surrounded by Indians. This group, according to Frances' memoir, was led by Chief Joseph, who was heading toward White Bird when they had spotted Isabella.

Thinking her time had come, Isabella stood there petrified. They asked if she wanted to go back to White Bird. She said no. Her watch and jewelry were taken, but Chief Joseph would not let them steal her ring which was "one ring that opened into several rings with a closing of clasped hands." They put Isabella on a horse and took her with them toward White Bird, away from Mount Idaho, despite her protestations. They finally put her down, showed her the direction to take, and told her to watch out for other Indians in the vicinity who would kill her if they caught her. Isabella believed she was released because they were grateful for all the times she had helped with sick Indian children or given food to Nez Perce in need.[16] Another version said some of the native women had done washing for Isabella and these women made fun of the braves who had taken her. At this point, Isabella was still about four miles from Mount Idaho and quickly hid in the timber again.

Local historian Charlotte Kirkwood's version was that, as the Nez Perce began to turn back from pursuing Perry's routed command, they met Isabella at the top of Whitebird Grade.

"She seemed wild and confused. They asked her if she wanted to go to Mount Idaho. She said 'Yes.' And talked in a rambling way about her children. An Indian tried to put her on his horse behind him. She pulled back when another Indian picked her up and succeeded in putting her on behind this Indian, who took her as near Mount Idaho as he dared for his own safety, then set her down, telling her to go on toward Mount Idaho."

The memory of Wounded Head, Husis Owyeen,

*Figure. 1.12 Historical sign at Mt. Idaho.
The town remains but is very small.
Photo by the author.*

amends, rather than contradicts, Isabella's version. Wounded Head, told his version to historian McWorter years later.[17] He had been drunk the night before the battle and unable to do much when the White Bird Battle began. He was asleep in the brush when his wife came and awakened him. A bit later, he rounded up some horses and headed after the fleeing soldiers but was too far behind to hope to catch them. He encountered an old Nez Perce man who gave him an ancient cap and ball pistol with only one bullet. Soon, he killed a soldier who raised his gun as if to shoot. He then traded pistols and took the dead soldier's cartridge belt. Wounded Head concluded once again that the fleeing soldiers were too far ahead. "We now turned back toward camp lower down the White Bird. While going on the trail I looked back and saw a bunch of Nez Perces. They called to me, 'Look ahead to the hillside. See what is coming toward you!' I looked. It was a white woman making her escape down the hillside. I rode to her. She made a sign that I do not kill her. I motioned her to get on the horse behind me. She did so and I turned back to the trail where the other Indians met me. I asked them to take charge of the woman, but they refused. With the woman I rode on down the trail, but not in view of the camp. I continued along the hill out of sight of the rest of the people, down to the gulch where I stopped. I think she was scared when I told her to get off to the ground. I instructed her to escape with her life, and I shook hands with her. She went and I rode back to camp."[18] Frances said years later that her "mother attributed her [second] release to many acts of kindness she had shown ... "[19]

Figure. 1.13 Close-up of Mt. Idaho sign. This was the area everyone of the prairie ran to for protection. Brown's hotel was here. The Mose Milner mentioned was also known as California Joe. Photo by the author.

Edward Robie, who had spent the

previous winter boarding at the Benedict home, questioned Frances when she arrived in Mount Idaho. He then rode out, unarmed, to look for Isabella. He rode first to the home of Charles Horton to see if he could borrow a gun. The watch dog would not let him in there, and later Horton was found slain in the home. Robie rode on to the Hughes place.

Isabella remembered the events this way: "I traveled all night, and just at dawn, reached a point near Henry Johnson's place on White-bird mountain. Seeing someone approaching, and supposing it to be an Indian, I hid in some willows near a straw stack."[20]

Near the Hughes ranch, Isabella saw her would-be rescuer, Ed Robie, but did not recognize him at that distance and hid behind a haystack. Luckily, he had seen her and called her name. "Imagine my surprise and delight when I realized that it was a friend coming to my rescue. The soldiers had reported me as left on the road, and Mr. Ruby (Robie), he who had left his gun in the care of my husband, hearing their story, and not being content to await the slow movement of the troops, had gone out to look for me."[21] He put her on his horse and led the horse back to Mount Idaho. At last, all of the surviving members of the Benedict family were safe and together.

Figure. 1.14 Mt. Idaho. This old but undated photo shows the town a few years after the Nez Perce War. It lost it status to Grangeville shortly after the war.
Photo from the collection of Deborah Starr.

Son, Grant Benedict, remembered that both he and his friend Hill Norton were sickened by an Indian scalp brought in by some Whites to prove they had killed an Indian. According to Adkison, this was the only scalp taken by either side in the whole conflict. Some accounts that say the Nez Perce women roamed the battle field after the fight mutilating corpses was simply racist nonsense. Perhaps troopers who died from wounds and then were in the June sun all day, looked mutilated.

When Isabella reached Mount Idaho she told her story to L. P. Brown, the hotel keeper who was trying to serve everyone at the makeshift fort and send out reports to area newspapers. She said that George Woodward and Peter Bertard had been killed at Baker's house, and her husband, and August Bacon were killed at her home. She believed that about 20 Indians made the attack.[22]

Ed Robie was commissioned a Captain in the Grangeville militia, but saw no more action in the war.

Back at Salmon River

The newspapers of the region picked up bits and pieces of the news and soon published both factual and unsubstantiated accounts of the conflict. On June 21, the *Statesman* of Boise listed four deaths plus "Samuel Benedict, wife and four children."[23] A dispatch out of Mount Idaho, dated June 30, told that Johnny Barber, a scout, and James Buchanan arrived there from Slate Creek with new information. They reported the houses and or stores of J. Manuel, Saml. Benedict, H. C. Brown, Bill George, Harry Mason, and others had been burned. They found and buried four bodies including Benedict's.[24] At least they thought it was Benedict's body.[25] In 1890, Louis Bocher submitted an affidavit that on June 20, 1877, he went to the Benedict home and saw Samuel's body lying in the creek behind the house, but did not attempt to retrieve it, and two weeks later, found some clothing buried in the ground but no sign of Benedict's body.[26]

After the Battle at Whitebird, the Nez Perce stayed in the general area for a number of days while General O. O. Howard moved in

"MOUNT IDAHO HOTEL". LOYAL P. BROWN, PRO. MT IDAHO, IDAHO TERR.

Figure. 1.15 Mount Idaho Hotel of L. P. Brown. Brown housed many refugees here and fed them. It was turned into a makeshift fort when the war began. Print from Elliot, Wallace W. "History of Idaho, The Territory: Showing Its Resources and Advantages". San Francisco: Wallace W. Elliot, 1884.

with more cavalry troops. Settlers, either on their own or as volunteers with the troops, circulated cautiously around the area. When the troopers crossed the Salmon River following the Nez Perce, "we found the trail of the Indians fresh, showing signs of hasty removal, leaving much plunder behind them. Here we found tons of flour and some clothing. One dress, trimmed in red velvet, was afterward identified by Mrs. Wood, of Slate Creek, as belonging to Mrs. Manuel." "Many caches were found here and opened. Among other things found was a little cradle quilt belonging to Mrs. Benedict."[27]

About the 30th of June: "Henry Brown and a few resolute men will attempt to go down to the mouth of White Bird to ascertain what has become of Brown's stock of goods, buildings, etc. A company of soldiers have gone to Salmon River through the gulch above White Bird. Indians have been seen to—day on all the prominent points overlooking the country near where the main body of troops are encamped.

The main body of troops, however, cannot be seen by the Indians. Theodore Swarts, Herman Faxon, Wm. Bloomer, John and Charley Crooks have particularly distinguished themselves in our late difficulties. Theo. Swarts even jumped his horse over the Indian who shot him. Johnny Barber, and in fact all of our boys, acted bravely during the contest. The bodies of Lieut. Theller and seven soldiers have been found and buried. Theller fought bravely and died from a shot through the head."[28]

Around this same time, the details of others from the White Bird area emerged as survivors trickled into various points of refuge. Six Frenchmen, including John Dumeck, Glotiney, G. Dizet, Le Bachebri, Victor Critien, and C. Jaiet, who lived on the south side of the Salmon below the mouth of Whitebird Creek, made their way into Lewiston by Sunday July 1.[29] Several of these individuals had seen the final attack on Samuel Benedict from a distance and were able to add

Figure. 1.16 Loyal Brown's Home at Mt. Idaho. Print from Elliot, Wallace W.
"History of Idaho, The Territory: Showing Its Resources and Advantages".
San Francisco: Wallace W. Elliot, 1884.

new details. On June 15 they fled their camp and secreted themselves in the canyons and brush near their homes. They changed locations frequently to avoid detection. Mr. Hussy, who was employed by the Benedicts, stayed with the group several days but finally ventured across the Salmon River and made his way safely to Mount Idaho. He had been at work on a ditch some distance from the Benedict house and had not been around when Samuel was killed.[30]

The Frenchmen saw Howard's command make its way down to the Salmon, and they thought they were safe at last. They headed toward the soldiers, but first encountered three Chinese men who told them every possible route to the soldiers was blocked by Nez Perce. The Frenchmen changed direction and headed down the River of No Return (Salmon River), about 20 miles to a cabin cut into the bank that could scarcely be seen. Once in there, they felt safe, but soon five Nez Perce with guns pointed were in front of the cabin. The Indians demanded and received the three shotguns the group had plus about $100. The Indians allowed the Frenchmen to cross to the north side of the river, and from there they headed toward Lewiston via Lake Waha.

The war was over in the Salmon River area in a few days and shifted toward, and then over, Lolo Pass to Montana. Howard's troopers pursued the Non-treaty Nez Perce. The war had left Camas Prairie and Isabella and her children were safe but fatherless.

Frances Benedict remembered: "After some months at Mount Idaho, when peace was restored, we moved to the little village of Grangeville, 20 miles from our White-bird house. Through the kindness of Mr. Crooks

Figure. 1.17 Nez Perce War historical sign on Camas Prairie. Several skirmishes and battles were fought before the Nez Perce headed to Montana. Photo by the author.

we were allowed to occupy the house near the Grange mill, built for the miller and his family, sharing with the Mitchell family, Mr. Mitchell being in charge at the time."[31] For Grant Benedict this had to be a very trying time. As Adkison pointed out, in a few days he went from school boy to orphan and breadwinner.[32] In the fall, he worked for Ed Robie, his future step-father, in the sawmill on Three Mile. On one occasion his presence of mind in turning off the water saved Robie who had gotten caught in the machinery.

Isabella filed a claim against James Bakers' estate for $766.25 total. She claimed to have labored for him from 15 January 1870 until 15 July 1876 and was due $390. She did washing, butter, sewing, flannel and cooking for three years from 1873 to 1875 and was due $210 for that. She also cleaned his house for $1.00 per week from 1876 to 15 June 1877 for a total due of $156.[33] Baker originally came to Idaho from California with Samuel Benedict and another man. He was an old family friend.

In 1890, Isabella stated that she had never once returned to the Salmon River homestead where she had lived with Samuel Benedict. Eventually, she lived within a few miles, and must have deliberately chosen not to go back to the site of her painful memories.

Isabella was now a widow with four children to support, and her home and store were destroyed. How had her life gotten her to this unanticipated situation? It was time for her to reflect on her earlier years.

Figure. 1.18 A sign on the Clearwater River honors Chief Looking Glass. Looking glass eventually joined the Non-treaties on their escape to Montana. Photo by the author.

In 1891, Erichson and Hanson advertised photos of sites involved in the Nez Perce War. They had operated a photography business in Moscow and had expanded to Grangeville. A few of the series of 46 photos are in various archives but complete sets have yet to be uncovered. Among the photos were: 24 - Benedict Ranch, mouth of White Bird. 28 - White Bird Battleground, where thirty-six U. S. Soldiers, under command of Col. Perry, were killed, June 17, 1877. 41 - Building in which the first Republican Convention in Idaho Territory was held. 42 - Mount Idaho, Hotel and Stockade. Other photos in the family archives owned by Deborah Starr may be from this set. Several photos of individual Benedict or Robie family members say the studio was in Moscow when the photos were actually taken at Grangeville. See the University of Idaho Special Collections web site under "Nez Perces Indian War Series '77," for more information on the history of the photographers and their studios.

End Notes

[1] Wilfong, *Following the Nez Perce Trail*, p. 86. The Benedict children present were eight-year-old Frances (Frankie) and one-and-a-half year-old Addie.

[2] Frances I. (Benedict) Shissler. *Bonners Ferry Herald*, Bonners Ferry, Idaho, 6 April 1939, p. 1, c.1 & 2, p. 6, c. 2 & 3.

[3] *The Florence Miner*, Florence, Idaho, 8 January 1898.

[4] Frances I. (Benedict) Shissler. *Bonners Ferry Herald*, Bonners Ferry, Idaho. 6 April 1939, p. 1, c.1& 2, p. 6, c. 2 & 3.

[5] Frances I. (Benedict) Shissler. *Bonners Ferry Herald*, Bonners Ferry, Idaho. 6 April 1939, p. 1, c.1& 2, p. 6, c. 2 & 3.

[6] The family kept the little shoe as a souvenir for years after this.

[7] Frances I. (Benedict) Shissler. *Bonners Ferry Herald*, Bonners Ferry, Idaho. 6 April 1939, p. 1, c.1 & 2, p. 6, c. 2 & 3.

[8] The best account of the trooper's journey to the head of White Bird Canyon may be found in McDermott's *Forlorn Hope*.

[9] McWhorter, *Hear Me My Chiefs, Hear Me My Chiefs: Nez Perce History and Legend*. Caldwell, Idaho: Caxton Printers, 1986. p. 235. According to General Howard, Mrs. Benedict and her children came out of the brush by the roadside after dawn when Perry's troops began to descend into White Bird Canyon. Howard's version was that, "The Indians had released her from her horrid confinement, and she was hiding against recapture by the more brutal." He was misinformed or perhaps speaking of later events.

[10] McDermott, *Forlorn Hope*, pp, 80-98. This is the best description and synopsis of the battle to date.

[11] Frances I. (Benedict) Shissler. *Bonners Ferry Herald*, Bonners Ferry, Idaho. 6 April 1939, p. 1, c.1 & 2, p. 6, c. 2 & 3. Charles Valentine Crooks was only a lad of 17 at this time. He was born in The Dalles, Oegon, in 1860. According to family lore related by Mike Peterson, Crooks used to race horses with the Nez Perce camped near Tolo Lake.

[12] Frances I. (Benedict) Shissler. *Bonners Ferry Herald*, Bonners Ferry, Idaho. 6 April 1939, p. 1, c.1 & 2, p. 6, c. 2 & 3. She calls the heroic soldier, "Mr. Semour," and says that years later he wrote the *Lewiston Tribune* for news of their where abouts.

[13] Frances I. (Benedict) Shissler. *Bonners Ferry Herald*, Bonners Ferry, Idaho. 6 April 1939, p. 1, c.1 & 2, p. 6, c. 2 & 3.

[14] Frances I. (Benedict) Shissler. *Bonners Ferry Herald*, Bonners Ferry, Idaho. 6 April 1939, p. 1, c.1& 2, p. 6, c. 2 & 3.

[15] Frances's story says that Mrs. Aram was the grandmother of Orrin Fitzgerald, of the University of Idaho.

[16] Charlotte M. Kirkwood, *The Nez Perce Indian War Under War Chiefs Joseph and Whitebird*. Grangeville: *Idaho County Free Press*, p. 32.

[17] Descendants of Wounded Head recall the honorable deed of this warrior to this day, and view it as an example of the Nez Perce resolve to avoid attacks on non-combatants.

[18] McWhorter, *Hear Me My Chiefs*, p. 240. Wounded Head said this was one good thing he did for the Whites. After he returned, he became good friends with Isabella. She gave him six dollars the first time she saw him after the war. He said she often invited him over to her house and treated him like a brother.

[19] Frances I. (Benedict) Shissler. *Bonners Ferry Herald*, Bonners Ferry, Idaho. 6 April 1939, p. 1, c.1& 2, p. 6, c. 2 & 3.

[20] Charlotte M. Kirkwood, *The Nez Perce Indian War Under War Chiefs Joseph and Whitebird*. Grangeville: *Idaho County Free Press*, p, 52.

[21] Charlotte M. Kirkwood, *The Nez Perce Indian War Under War Chiefs Joseph and Whitebird*. Grangeville: *Idaho County Free Press*, p. 52.

[22] *The Teller*, Lewiston, 30 June 1877, p. 1, c. 3 & 4. *Tri-Weekly Statesman*, Boise, Idaho, 28 June 1877, p. 1, c. 1

[23] *Tri-Weekly Statesman*, Boise, Idaho, 21 June 1877, p. 1, c. 1.

[24] *Tri-Weekly Statesman*, Boise, Idaho, 14 July 1877, p. 2, c. 1.

[25] Most later records say that Benedict's body was never recovered. Son Grant Benedict examined a skeleton found near Horseshoe Bend a few miles from the site of the old Benedict store. He believed they were Indian remains. See Robert Bailey, *River of No Return*, 1935, p. 205.

[26] This was submitted with the material to the court of claims. See McDermott, *Forlorn Hope*, p. 18.

[27] Charlotte M. Kirkwood, *The Nez Perce Indian War Under War Chiefs Joseph and Whitebird*. Grangeville: *Idaho County Free Press*, p. 8.

[28] *Idaho Tri-Weekly Statesman*, Boise, Idaho, 7 July 1877, p. 3, c. 2.

[29] *The Teller*, Lewiston, Idaho, Saturday 7, July, 1877, p. 1, c. 3 & 4.

[30] Charlotte M. Kirkwood, *The Nez Perce Indian War Under War Chiefs Joseph and Whitebird*. Grangeville: *Idaho County Free Press*, p. 47.

[31] Frances I. (Benedict) Shissler. *Bonners Ferry Herald*, Bonners Ferry, Idaho. 6 April 1939, p. 1, c.1 & 2, p. 6, c. 2 & 3.

[32] J. Loyal Adkison, "Benedict Family closely Related to Early Idaho County History," *Idaho County Free Press*, Grangeville, Idaho, 27 March 1952.

[33] Notes in family history file with no citation.

2

ISABELLA'S EARLY LIFE

Birth to living at Freedom, Idaho: 1847-1864

ISABELLA WAS BORN ON November 26, 1847 at Staten Island, New York to the newly arrived Irish family of John N. Kelly.[1] The family then moved to Tompkinsville, New York, which is a neighborhood in northeastern Staten Island, New York City, and may not have involved a lengthy move at all. Here Mary Ann (28 March 1852), Sarah (6 July 1853) and Francis (Frank) were born. According to William Olson's research, they left little Frank with relatives and took the Panama route to California in the 1850s. Others say they went to California in 1849 around the horn, but this would not have allowed time for the three siblings of Isabella to be born in New York, which they clearly were. According to Sarah's obituary, the trip was on the ship "Sierra Nevada," and took 21 days. A young ward, Elizabeth G. Castello, came with Sarah Kelly.[2] Her obituary, decades later, said they all took the narrow-gauge railroad across the Isthmus of Panama.[3] Family lore is that Elizabeth's mother knew the Kelly family. Her husband had left and she died in childbirth, but first asked the Kellys to raise her daughter. Elizabeth was 11 and one-half years old on the U.S. Census while the extended Kelly family was in Portland, Oregon.

Isabella's mother was Sarah O'Donnell of Donegal Castle in County Cork, Ireland. In San Francisco, Father John Kelly was associated with William C. Ralston in some sort of real estate business and once owned the land where the Palace Hotel was later located.

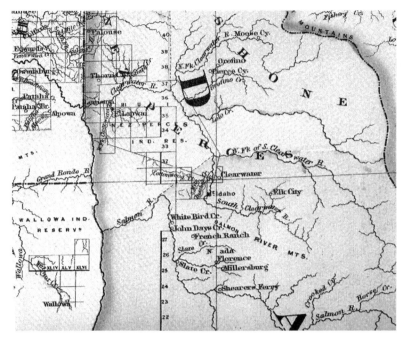

Figure. 2.1 Map of the region. John Day Creek should be south of Slate Creek, not north. This historical map shows the locations most important to these events.

William Chapman Ralston made money in the Nevada Comstock Lode and built many buildings in San Francisco. He also founded the Bank of California. Building the Palace Hotel drained the resources of Ralston and his bank. After the business association there ended, the Kelly family went to Portland where son, John James, was born and father John operated the first St. James Hotel. They sold the hotel and tried ranching on the Yuba River, but soon sold that and went to the Snake River at an unnamed location. December of 1861 saw a devastating flood on the Yuba River that, among other damage, destroyed the bridge at Simpson's Ferry.[4] It was fortunate they had already moved away.

The Kelly family had no luck at their next stop. The Columbia River flood of early 1862 destroyed their property, according to Olson. A flood on the Columbia would certainly have backed up into the Snake, or the Snake had its own separate flood. The exact chronology of the Kelly wanderings is not known, but the winter of

1861-62 was one of the worst ever known in several respects. At Oregon City, Oregon, rain fell almost continuously during November, creating a great flood.[5] The Willamette River had one of its greatest floods, and floods reached from Northern California to Eastern Oregon. Portland, and the Deschutes River area both suffered great floods. By January, the swollen Columbia was closed by ice. In February, the newspaper in Walla Walla reported they had not received any news from Portland for 53 days.[6]

After this, the Kelly family caught the great Salmon River gold fever and headed to Florence with many others. There, the family with 14-year-old Isabella, 10-year-old Mary Ann, nine-year-old Sarah, 2-year-old John James, and apparently 13-year-old Elizabeth Castello settled down to make their fortune.

At Florence, Kelly operated a store with S. Lindsay, according to family legend and property records. A sheriff's sale held on 8 December 1862 was at the property of Muller, Swartz and Nelson described as between the property of George Popham and Kelly and Lindsay. Records indicate that Kelly did purchase a lot 20 by 100 feet from S. George, H. Holbrook and O. S. Simmons on the east side of Main Street for $1,500. He also bought a half interest in the Madden and Young Saloon. George Popham was the father of Jeanette Popham, life-long friend of Isabella. The two teenage girls must have been neighbors in Florence, and the only girls in the camp in their age group. Jeanette's life and Isabella's, beginning at this time, were intertwined in many ways through many events.

Florence, Idaho County

Gold! Gold! Gold! It is a powerful word now, but in the 19th Century just a whisper of it drove men insane with lust. Prospectors would go to Hell itself, wrestle the Devil, endure any hardship, risk life and limb for the soul-shriveling intoxication the precious metal promised. Like worker bees on spilled nectar, they literally swarmed to the source of each rumor of gold and dug into the ground till both it and they were exhausted. Then, they would immediately head off to the next spot with just wild rumors as the sole incentive. High in the mountains of Idaho County, before the Territory of Idaho was formed and it was still part of Washington, the dream of wealth and the fulfillment of that dream collided to a degree rarely ever before recorded. After the initial find of gold in Pierce, miners spread out in every direction to seek the mother lode. On August 12, 1861, two months after the first finds at nearby Elk City, three miners found the first gold at Florence. Mining work began in late summer of 1861, but winter soon halted work. For a few short months in 1862 the dream blossomed; men dug, panned, and rocked simple cradles while their ever-growing hoards of $13-an-ounce gold fulfilled their wildest fantasies. By the middle of 1863, only the hard-core believers in Florence still clung to the area. The easily taken placer gold did not last long.

Despite its short life, Florence produced a plethora of stories, legends, tales, short memoirs, gross exaggerations, and nostalgia. There were also down-right lies made up to make the place still more colorful.

By October, 1861 of that first season, Jack Morrow Phillips left Florence with 250 pounds of gold. By November, goods were being packed in at $1 per pound to sustain the miners through the snow and bitter cold season. An express man returning to Walla Walla on December 19 reported snow two-and-a-half-feet deep and 1,000 miners in Florence toughing it out.[7]

In March of 1862—March is nowhere near the end of winter in the mountain country—Florence ran out of whiskey. Two men made a snowshoe trek to the low land to procure something to ease this dangerous situation, but they died on the trail back when they drank too freely from their kegs of raw alcohol. Another man in camp found a

Figure. 2.2 Fabulous Florence sign. Historical marker describes the gold camp. Photo by the author.

half-gallon jug of whiskey that winter and sold it for $50 after water-
ing it considerably.[8] There was a definite demand for something to
feed the inner man.

The Yreka, California, newspaper at first preached that the Salmon River gold mines were a fraud, or at least not very valuable. They
wanted their citizens to stay in
Northern California. Eventually, they gave in and seemed to
bend to the inevitable demand for
information on the trip to Florence. In early April of 1862, they
published a long article by T. R.
Olney based mostly on the hand-
book for travelers to the mines
written by Hutchings and Rosen-
field.[9] Olney said he had gone to

*Figure. 2.3 Old Florence sign. This
was the original site of the town but the
new growth of trees makes identification
of individual historic sites nearly
impossible. Photo by the author.*

the mines from Salt Lake City and had stopped along the way to
prospect the Payette, Owyhee and Malheur rivers, among others, but
his party was driven away by the "mean, thieving and decidedly hostile bands of Snake Indians." He did describe the three main routes
from Lewiston to the mines. Across Camas Prairie the distance was
117 miles; via a middle route, it was 98 miles through rough country;
and going first to Elk City, one had a choice of trails. The difficult trail
out of Elk City was only 145 miles; the packer's favorite trail from
there was 155 miles.

The Florence area included several town sites—sometimes with
only a few structures and no more than three or four miles apart—
named Nevada City, Millerstown, Meadow Creek, Baboon Gulch,
Pioneer Gulch, Mason's Gulch, Neal's Gulch, Ureka, Florence City,
Freedom, and others. Olney also said the previous winter was much
worse than the preceding two, and recommended that leaving from
San Francisco before the middle of May was "only time and money
thrown away."

As the urge to go to the new gold claims became a fever, the satirists began to write numerous poems and songs about the experience. The following appeared in Yreka in May of 1862:

Salmon River Dixie

Away up North, where runs the Salmon,
There's lots of gold—'tis no darned gammon;
Get away, get away, way up north to Salmon
So Yank and Pike, Kentuck and I,
Are going up there our luck to try;
Get away, get away, way up north to Salmon
Then I wish I was on Salmon!
    Huppa, Mula!
On Salmon's site I'll strike my pile,
And go it strong on Salmon;
    Away, away, away up north on Salmon.

I have got my outfit all complete,
Selfrising flour, and lots of meat;
    Get away, &c.
Three Navy Colts, and rifled gun,
With which to make the Indians run;
    Get away, &c.
O, I wish I was on Salmon!
    Huppa, Mula!
With pick and pan I'll take my stand,
And strike it big on Salmon;
    Away, &c.

The song was much longer but this conveys the idea.

Another song by Max Irwin was used by a band of Negro minstrels at Portland and sung to the tune of "Jordan."[10]

I looked to the North and I looked to the South
And I saw the Californians a coming.

With their picks, pans and shovels on their backs,
They were traveling their way up to Salmon.

Then save your money boys to pay your way thro'
Two to one on Salmon against Cariboo,
Don't be too haty and gert into a fever,
For you'll all make a fortune up in Salmon river.

We left California with a hundred pound pack,
And rest on the Siskiyou Mountains,
We took a drink of red-eye and started on the track,
For its a hard road to travel up to Salmon.

The song was much longer and gave details of how difficult the journey really was.[11]

The people of Yreka never tired of hearing of the new mines. In late May, a published letter from Nathan Wheeler said the mines were rich but limited, and Bradley and Preston Dean were building a saloon in Florence.[12] In June of 1862, the Yreka newspaper quoted a Mr. Quivey, saying that "if one had a $2 claim in Siskiyou (County, California) he was better off then going to the Salmon River." A more balanced report the next month said Florence was about twice of the size of Deadwood [of Siskiyou County] and the amount of gold coming out had already dropped due to lack of water for mining and lack of gold.[13]

Dr. George C. Furber, formerly of Yreka, wrote from Florence in late April 1862 that it would be two more months before the road to the Salmon River mines would be open. The winter left more snow "than has ever before been seen by white men on this coast."[14] Furber placed a legal advertisement in the Yreka newspaper all the way from Florence revoking the power of attorney he had given to E. Steele, esq. and giving it to Joseph Hawkins instead.[15]

When Furber, returned to town from Florence in October 1862, he mentioned the ill health and near starvation there the winter before, and the Yreka newspaper mentioned that the town of Florence was named for one of his children.[16] There has always been some controversy about the origin of that name. Furber applied for bankruptcy soon after his return and became the head clerk in a drug store.[17]

On November 8, 1862, the people of Lewiston—specifically the Members of the Lewiston Protective Association, Idaho's original vigilance committee—hanged Dave English, Nelson Scott, and William Peoples for the robbery of J. G. Berry and his brother of $1,200. The three had run in various directions after the robbery but were rounded up; Peoples was at Walla Walla, Scott near by at Dry Creek, and English at Wallula on the Columbia River. Back in Yreka, California, this was significant news.[18] English had lived there and made his living breaking colts. He left a wife and family at Corvallis and another wife at Walla Walla. Peoples was the brother of a celebrated circus rider and had lived in Siskiyou County briefly. Nelson Scott formerly resided at Scott Valley, Siskiyou County, and left a wife and child. His wife and parents were perceived as good citizens. In fact, a summons for Nelson Scott had been published in the Yreka Journal in May of 1862 because his wife was suing him for his divorce and seeking custody of their child.[19]

Figure 2.4 Historical sign describes the mining in the area around Florence. Gold was the magnet that drew the first settlers to Florence and the surrounding towns. Photo by the author.

In 1911, John Riordan, who had lived in Florence before moving to Lewiston, related his memory of the lynching.[20] The men were held in a room that had formerly been a saloon. The man in charge of the prisoners went to Riordan's cabin to borrow his only three coffee cups so they could serve the prisoners. The next day as Riordan and his partner left to go up the Clearwater fishing, they remembered the cups and went to fetch them.

"Riordan started over to the cabin where the prisoners were installed, and looking in the window he saw all three hanging from the inside of the roof, the shakes having been removed to afford room for the ropes. ... One of the men, he says, hung with his feet so close to the floor that one could not put his hands between them and the floor but all three were dead, hanging in a row. He immediately notified the nearest neighbor, and was then asked to assist in removing the copses. This, he says, he declined to do until the coroner came. This was only one case of the vigilantes taking matters into their own hands, Mr. Riordan says, but that morning his appetite was destroyed for coffee."[21]

Another man was found hanging in a tree on the Florence road about this same time who was also erroneously identified as Charley Harper. It was someone else, since Harper was killed at the end of the year in Washington Territory. Some believe these hangings motivated Henry Plummer to head into Montana, but he was already

Figure. 2.5 Florence Idaho. Idaho State Historical Society. 1. Masonic Hall 13. Dance Hall, 3. Cherokee Bob's Saloon. 4. Red-headed Cynthia's House. 5. McKensie's General Store. Photo from Idaho Historical Society.

east of the Rockies by then. Once again the neat, simple explanation was simply wrong. The Lewiston vigilance group drove out about 200 during the winter of 1862-63 and then dissolved.[22] A lynching at Lewiston foreshadowed a later event that more directly involved Isabella.

On June 1, 1862, Seth Jones and his wife, Jane, arrived in Florence. She was the first woman to use the new Milner Trail from Mount Idaho to Florence, and the whole family was not charged a toll in honor of the event.[23] There were other trails into Florence, but this provides some evidence that the Kelly family had not yet reached the town at that time.

Samuel Benedict

Benedict was born in Shannonville, Prince Edward County, Ontario, Canada on 20 August 1835. Benedict arrived in San Francisco on 21 May 1852 from Panama via Acapulco on the brig "Dudley." According to Idaho Genealogical Society records, Benedict mined in California and was trained as a blacksmith. Benedict was in California during the Rogue River War of 1855 and participated to some degree in the conflict. The Rogue River War actually re-erupted in

Figure. 2.6 Florence, Idaho. Another view of old Florence. Several buildings have been razed by this time. Photo from Idaho State Historical Society.

October 1855, when a swarm of men from Jacksonville, a mining town in the Rogue River Valley of southwestern Oregon Territory, massacred at least 28 Indians encamped in the vicinity of the Table Rock Reservation.

That and several subsequent attacks on Rogue River Valley natives were intended to spark a war that would employ miners, unable to mine owing to a long dry spell, as paramilitary "volunteers." Acquiring more land from the Indians was not a factor.

Leaders of the southwestern Oregon Indian people had already inked treaties relinquishing the lion's share of their homelands. The Rogue River tribes had endured the aggression of Oregon Trail and California Gold Rush immigrants and had put up stiff resistance to them in the early 1850s. The U.S. Army inflicted numerous punitive assaults against the Rogue River natives, beginning in 1851.

Joel Palmer, Oregon Superintendent of Indian Affairs, and General John E. Wool, the U.S. Army commander on the Pacific Coast, actually opposed the new hostilities. But General Lane, the territorial delegate in Washington and a heavyweight in the ruling Democratic Party, asserted himself in favor of war, and anticipated receiving swift remuneration for war claims.

Indian people who chose to fight, led by Tecumtum (Chief John) of the Etch-ka-taw-wah band, took refuge in the Coast Range. They effectively repelled assaults, most notably in the Battle of Hungry Hill at the end of October 1855. Others chose to place themselves under the protection of regular troops at Fort Lane, commanded by Captain Andrew Smith. They were removed in January 1856, to the Grand Ronde Reservation in northwestern Oregon.

In February 1856, the natives in the mountains brought the fight down the Rogue River to the Pacific Coast, apparently to buy time to find food following a harsh winter. They nearly cleared the coast of non-natives, but in May they came under attack from two directions.

Regular army troops moved north along the coast from Crescent City, California, and met little opposition. Most of the combatants submitted to that unit's commander, apparently because they believed that the army would protect them from more predatory volunteer troops.

The volunteers, meanwhile, came down the Rogue toward the coast, and at Big Meadow attacked natives who had already submitted to the regulars.

The followers of Tecumtum put up their final resistance at Big Bend on the river, where they nearly overcame regular troops who

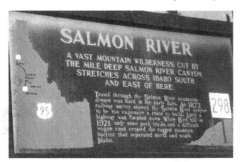

Figure. 2.7 Salmon River historical sign.
Photo by the author.

were guarding a prisoner-of-war camp. In 1856, in a ghostly reminiscence of the Cherokees' Trail of Tears, between 900 and 1,000 natives were compelled to relocate to the Siletz and Grand Ronde reservations west of present-day Salem, Oregon.

Some were obliged to trudge up the coast to their new domicile, the Coast Reservation, on the central coast. There was fierce resistance to the removal because people thought they would be allowed to stay at Table Rock.

Exactly when Benedict quit the war and left for the Idaho mines is not known. The story is that in California he met James Baker, and the men went to Idaho together with "Indian Joe." The men were partners in a 60-mule pack outfit. They got loads of freight at either Umatilla, the head of steamboat navigation, Boise, or Lewiston, and took the loads to Florence and Warren. Pete Smith bought their

Figure. 2.8 Trail sign near Florence. The road between Florence and Warren. On this trail the posse of 1863 killed Fat Jack and Nesselrod.
Photo by the author.

first load into Florence for $5,000 gold dust. The sale was made at Resort (later known as Burgdorf Hot Springs). Smith was buying for Miller's Camp, a sort of mining company. The purchase called for everything except the mules and halters. Arch Dyer's father witnessed the sale. The packers then went back to Umatilla for another load.

Benedict was also given credit for operating the first blacksmith shop in Lewiston. He became good friends with Joaquin Miller who was operating a pack train into Florence. Miller became famous as a writer.

Benedict had been in the Florence area prospecting before 5 July of 1862 when he filed nine quartz claims in partnership with eight other men. Family tradition says Benedict ran a store in Florence. Other reports say he also had a blacksmith shop. The sparse records fail to corroborate this but he did own a 20 by100 foot lot he

Figure. 2.9 Portrait drawing of Samuel Benedict. Photocopy from the collection of Deborah Starr.

bought for $1,500 from S. George, H. Holbrook and O. S. Simmons on the east side of main street.[24] He also had a half interest in lot 1, block 3 on the corner of Main and Miners Streets known as Madden and Young's Saloon.

The Great New Year's Gunfight in Florence

In the East, President Lincoln was issuing the final Emancipation Proclamation on New Year's Day of 1863; the Civil War hostilities were quiet for the winter, but preparations were under way for the next year that was destined to decide the ultimate outcome. Florence, Idaho, had its own hostile factions, loosely related to the struggle in

Figure. 2.10 Florence Cemetery sign. The cemetery at Florence is about all that is left to see. This tells the story of Cherokee Bob. Photo by the author.

the East, and they were in no way reluctant to wage battle in the snow. Californians with Unionist ideas and paroled Confederate veterans had vastly different views of the world.

The New Year of 1863 was properly celebrated January 1, not December 31, in Florence with a great ball. A break in the winter tedium and a chance to alleviate cabin fever were universally desired. Many miners had musical training and it was easy to organize a makeshift band. In packer Herman Reinhart's memory, the dance was a Masonic ball.[25] There was a Masonic Hall in Florence but it was an informal lodge, as no official lodge was ever chartered there.

Fourteen year-olds, Jeanette Popham and Isabella Kelly, must have been anxious all day if not for several days in anticipation of the ball.[26] Certainly they had on their finest dresses and shoes, and best hairdos. The town offered few if any diversions for teenagers—a category of citizens not even recognized in that era.

Wilton (Red Face Bill or Poker Bill) Willoughby, in the stead of Cherokee Bob Talbot, and Cynthia Ewing, representatives of the worldly portion of the camp, were at the first great ball in Florence along with Jenny Popham, Isabella Kelly, Jakie Williams, Rube Robbins, and dozens, if not hundreds, of lonesome miners.[27] The two social outcasts, Cynthia and Willoughby, were refused admittance by Jakie Williams and Orlando "Rube" Robbins, according to one story.[28] According to another more detailed version, with Cynth decked out like a Christmas tree, she and Willoughby entered the hall. They were met with scowls and evidence of disgust on every hand. The women gathered in groups, discussed the situation, and quickly threatened to leave and demand their money back if Cynthia remained. One may envision Jeanette and Isabella being called over to the indignant group with only a minimal understanding of what motivated their mothers and the other women to be so upset that they were willing to storm out of the eagerly anticipated ball. The management committee held a conference. Robbins and Williams, the floor managers, had a duty to perform. Williams whispered words to Willoughby, who departed quietly with Red-headed Cynth. Back at Bob's saloon, they told Cherokee Bob their tale of rejection. He considered this a personal insult and declared vengeance on Robbins, and in particular Jakie Williams. "I'll kill him," he swore.

How reminiscent this seems of the tale in "The Outcasts of Poker Flat" in which the fictitious town was cleansed by driving out all the gamblers and prostitutes. The conflict was not just the respectable against the disrespectable; it was also Northern and Western values against the genteel traditions of the South. Incidentally and ironically, the gambler in Bret Hart's classic tale was modeled on Cherokee Bob.

This confrontation led to a classic western shootout in the icy streets of Florence the next day.[29] According to historian Gibbs, "Jakie" Williams was a rival saloon owner. He was described as an athletic man, a former California law officer, and a determined enemy of the robbers.[30] When he learned he was the object of Cherokee Bob's wrath, he sought to avoid a fight. The next morning, Williams slipped out of his saloon and sought refuge at one house after the other. Cherokee Bob and Willoughby, armed to the teeth, were always close behind. Rube Robbins and Cherokee Bob nearly clashed during that day when they met accidentally on the street, but Mr. John Keenan, Deputy Sheriff of Idaho County, intervened and prevented bloodshed at that moment.[31] When Jakie could dodge no more, he reentered his saloon just as his pursuers fired at him. He grabbed a shotgun from behind the bar, and the stalked became the stalker.

By this time, many people in Florence must have been aware of the situation. Few miners, if any, were at work this time of year; saloons were full; rumors spread with the speed of a blizzard's wind.

Was the impending tragedy awaited or even suspected in the Popham hotel? Did Jeanette suspect that the man she had developed her little crush on would soon face an opponent who had killed many such men before? Was Isabella aware of what was happening? The answer would only be speculation.

In the late afternoon twilight and cold of winter, the parties finally faced each other in front of the Bank Exchange Saloon. Williams spied Willoughby coming around a corner and dropped him with revolver fire and possibly a blast from the shotgun—16 slugs (or 14 in other accounts) entered Willoughby's body. Willoughby returned fire, tried to run, but when he had exhausted his 12 shots he fell and pleaded, "For God's sake, don't shoot any more. I'm dying now."[32] To the consternation of no one, he fulfilled his prediction and died momentarily.

At this point Jakie's friends, particularly Rube Robbins, entered the fray. One version said Cherokee Bob was about to fire his pistol when he was shot with a rifle from a nearby building. An alternate version said Cherokee fired until his pistols were empty and was brought down by a ball fired from an opposite window. Defenbach said that an informal posse consisting of most of Florence aided Williams.[33] Five shots hit Cherokee Bob. He died a few days later in his saloon where his mortally wounded body had been carried. Rube Robbins deserves the credit for the killing, not some nameless sniper. Before he died, Bob said Jakie and Rube were "both brave men but Jakie always steps aside to get clear of the smoke of his revolver, while Rube pushes through it and keeps coming, getting closer with each shot."[34] Another version said Cherokee died

Figure. 2.11 A photo of the original Cherokee Bob grave marker at the Centennial Museum in Grangeville. Photo by the author.

thinking he had killed Jakie Williams, and his last words were for his brother in Lewiston: "Tell my brother I have killed my man and gone on a long hunt."

Bob and Willoughby were buried in the frozen Florence cemetery among a host of unmarked graves.[35] The Portland newspaper called Henry Tolbert (sic) "one of the most murderously desperate men that has ever figured on the coast."[36] Nearly 40 years later, a newspaper account remembered Talbot and Willoughby as highwaymen, horse thieves and "Knights of the Road." Talbot was also remembered as a "chief" among the "road agents."[37] For some inexplicable reason, *Idaho: American Guide Series* said he was "slain by another bandit as notorious as himself."[38] That was patently untrue. Some writers view the fight as the first definitive action taken by the new Vigilance Committee of Florence.

Justice of the Peace Rand vindicated the winners.[39] According to historian James Hawley, "the thanks of the community were extended to Williams and Robbins for having rid the town of two of the professional bad men."[40] Apparently, the fine reputations of the winners and the vile reputations of the losers made for an easy legal decision on a frontier trying to rid itself of gun-toting toughs. Accounts of the fight that fail to mention Rube Robbins were refuted by his status—no one else's—as codefendant in the court case. The actual Docket Book from Florence has survived and with a few more details.[41] The hearing was held on January 6. before Justice Jasper Rand in the case of Territory of Washington vs. J. D. Williams and Orlando Robbins. J. S. Gray was the attorney for the defendants, "who demanded an investigation into the matter of the killing," and he examined 11 witnesses including Sheriff John Keenan. The court decided Jakie and Rube acted in self-defense, were justified, and ordered them released.

The Portland, Oregon, Morning Oregonian said that on January 7, the weather at Florence was mild, snow was two-feet-deep, little mining was being done by the 800 men there, and oh yes, "Cherokee Bob and his mate hunted industriously for a fight, and at last found it."[42]

One version of the gun fight told by alleged witness, Barney Owsley, said Red-headed Cynth did not want Cherokee to commit murder and she removed the caps from each chamber of his ball and
cap pistol, rendering him defenseless.[43] Maybe, but probably not.
If Cherokee's revolvers had repeatedly failed to fire everyone would
have noted the fact. Owsley remembered this in his 90th year and had
a few details confused. When he gave the interview in 1937, he described Florence as currently a "city of bats and ghosts." He also said
there were no respectable women at the New Year's dance as none
had yet arrived in town. Cynthia went south to Placerville or Idaho
City next to re-connect with her former lover, William Mayfield. She
reunited with him—just before he too was gunned down. Mayfield
was killed in August of 1863. In an unexpected twist, the shooter,
Evans, was arrested by J. D. Williams, the newly elected sheriff of
Boise Basin. Historian Defenbach said Cynth swore to kill Mayfield's
murderer but instead stayed in Placerville's red light district.[44] Supposedly she continued her wanton ways and ruined many a man as
she sought to survive and endure on the frontier with no capital, save
her sexuality. In actuality, she next went to Walla Walla to continue
to work in the sex trade, and to be divorced by her long-suffering
husband. Eventually she went back to Florence.

With Cherokee Bob dead, James Mitchell reappeared on the scene
and asserted his ownership of the Boomerang Saloon.[45] Cherokee had
intimidated Mitchell into relinquishing it for free. It was described
as on the west side of Miner Street, lot 88 of block 9, with a 30-foot
frontage. He appeared in court and swore that Henry Talbotte (sic)
had seized the property, and swore to his rightful ownership and his
willingness to defend the title. Jonas Brown, County Auditor, swore
to Mitchell's identity.[46]

On 27 January 1863, Frank Whittier wrote home to Yreka with
a highly factual report on the situation.[47] He talked of traveling into
Florence on snowshoes, which from his description sound more like
cross-country skis. There were 6 to 7 hundred miners there, and 14
women excluding those in the "cradles." Among the "women" must

have been Jeanette and Isabella. Most of the people, including sheriff John Keenan and Deputy Jim Judge, were from Siskiyou. There were, in contrast to the previous winter, plenty of provisions. The nearby mining camp of Warren was hard to reach and only about 200 were wintering there. "We have had several shooting affairs, all of which you have no doubt seen published. Florence has ended the career of many desperadoes—next season will be more quiet." Large gray wolves were numerous and killing beef cattle nearby. "Strychnine is about to be administered."

In 1863, Benedict earned a reputation and a place in the historical record when he was in charge of a group of men sent out by the Miner's Association of Florence to apprehend a suspected robber of sluices.[48] The Association was a vigilante group that renewed their effort at ridding Florence of criminals after the Cherokee Bob altercation. "Fat Jack"—no other name was recorded for the man who won his ironic nickname because of his tall, lean, cadaverous appearance—had previously been ordered out of the camp by president Bill Moomau and the other members of the Association under suspicion of looting unguarded sluices in Bear Track Gulch. Jack went to Walla Walla according to historian Langford, who described him as "belonged to that class of negative scoundrels, whose love for crime is confined by fear to petty thefts."[49] Jack brooded over his expulsion and finally returned to Florence. Three weeks later, or in other memories two months, Jack returned, and the Association decided to bring him in for trial. The Executive Committee told him to retrace

his steps or be hanged. He went door to door seeking shelter from the storm but no one would let him in so he headed toward Warren. Benedict's posse caught up with Jack where the trail to Warren intersects Sand Creek. Jack was

Figure. 2.12 Cherokee Bob's current grave marker at Florence. Photo by the author.

in a cabin owned by a Mr. Nesselrode. He had been given a place to sleep by the fire, and with Nesselrode's hired man, there were three in the cabin. When ordered out, Jack fired a shot at the posse, some said. Langford said two men, who admitted they had no authority but still demanded the surrender of Jack, awakened Nesselrode. Western hospitality decreed Jack could not be given up. The posse fired several volleys into the cabin, including two blasts of shot from double barrel shot guns, until no shots were returned. The hired man was safe, but Jack and Nesselrode had been shot. When the posse entered, Jack was found dead, and the innocent host Nesselrode mortally wounded.[50]

The Yreka, California, Semi-Weekly Journal said the man killed was William H. Tomen who had been threatening citizens. Unrestrained vigilantism batted 50 percent that day. In Langford's self-serving account in his book, the "criminals" who killed Nesselrode were never discovered and the Vigilantes themselves were indignant about his killing.

In March of 1863, the new territory of Idaho was formed, and Congress ratified the new treaty with the Nez Perce. The reservation was now only 700,000 acres, and divided by new political boundaries. Ownership of the Wallowa Valley in Oregon was vague. Chief Lawyer signed for all the Nez Perce, though nothing in Nez Perce tradition gave him the right to do so. Those who were not in favor of the agreement were henceforth known as Non-treaty Nez Perce. The newly-wed Benedicts had other interests than these details, but the ramifications of the treaty would haunt the family years later.

The Colorful Characters of Florence

In April of 1910, Frank R. Coffin of Boise invited everyone in Boise who, as himself, had been in Florence 48 years before in 1862, to come to his home for a meal and a get-together.[51] Len Richardson was out of town, Relf Bledsoe was too sick, and Coffin did not know that James H. Hawley had been at Florence and accidentally did not invite him. The list of those who did accept the invitation, though, was impressive: Judge Jonas W. Brown, John Hailey, Stephen Sisk,

I. Tiner, Fred Hottes, James H. Hart, and C. E. Higby all came to tell stories of their days in that special place. Life in Florence was the initiation rite that made pioneers of many lifetime Idahoans.

Captain Relf Bledsoe told his reminiscences of the early days in 1909.[52] In 1861, Bledsoe, of the firm Malphy, Creighton & Bledsoe, had just left Lewiston with a pack train of supplies heading for Elk City when he met Nate Smith at Cold Spring on Craig's Mountain. Relf decided to drop half of his goods at Florence, only 70 miles away, and much closer than Elk City. Bledsoe said when news of the gold finds at Florence spread, miners came from all directions. The route was up the mountains from the Salmon River. At White Bird Creek, Nez Perce headman, "Eagle of the Light," and his warriors held the pass for several days and stopped the miners. Another Nez Perce Chief, "Old Billy," came with a hundred warriors to talk to Bledsoe at Cold Spring and said they were friendly to the Whites and would see that the miners could go through. Bledsoe gave that group 10 sacks of flour and a lot of tobacco as a sign of friendship.

At Florence, Bledsoe saw two men on Baboon gulch melting water to operate their gold rocker, and thereby taking out a pint of gold dust per day. Everything sold for a dollar a pound, according to Bledsoe's memory. He often saw men packing in supplies on their backs in loads of 100 or 125 pounds. At Slate Creek, Bledsoe met James Baker, who was a well-known packer by that time. He figured in Isabella's life later on the Salmon River. Eventually, Relf bought a pack train of 45 mules and five riding horses for $5,500.

One time Bledsoe encountered 2 desperadoes—Peoples and English, who were later lynched at Lewiston—on the trail when he had $10,000 in gold dust that he was taking to Lewiston. Bledsoe saw them coming and had his shotgun across his knees on top of the saddle. They greeted him pleasantly. Relf told then to both ride on the same side of him, the side facing the muzzle of the gun. They said he was too cautious but he would not waiver. Next, they asked for whiskey. Relf said they could have some but they had to put down their guns and stay on one side of him. After a drink, the highwaymen told him to go ahead. He told them to go ahead and as he would not change his mind, they went on toward Mount Idaho. Bledsoe then rode through the timber to avoid an ambush and made Lewiston without further incident.

Among the stories exchanged that night so many years later in Boise was Jimmy Hart's tales of life in Florence.

"A little town called Nevada was the only place to buy any snake bite medicine and they were well patronized. I paid Dr. Smith $250 for a small bottle of Perry Davis' Pain Killer for our cabin mate. The poor devil had the scurvy. We did not know what to do about scurvy only to eat raw potatoes and they were like diamonds at $1 a pound. When I got back to the cab-in the poor devil was dead with no chance to test my expensive medicine."

Alonzo F. Brown wrote an oft-quoted memoir of his days in Florence.[53] After trying some very physically demanding mining, Alonzo unexpectedly went into the retail sales busi-

Figure. 2.13 *Cherokee Bob marker.*
Photo by the author.

ness in partnership with D. W. Stearns, who had just brought in a pack train of goods and needed someone to sell them. [54] Brown took in $7,000 the first week in business. Brown remembered: "The men had a habit of getting drunk at the saloons and shooting into stores and tents as they went by. I slept in the store on the floor, and to protect myself from the stray bullets fired by drunken men I piled up a stack of flour as wide as my bed and about four feet high and made down my bed behind the flour."

He also reported: "The town was filled with the worst element of the Pacific Coast, and thieves and gamblers from the East. The saloons and gambling houses were wide open night and day and a man was killed nearly every night." Historian Ronald Limbaugh described the saloon of Cyrus Skinner as a rendezvous point for road agents.[55] His property was eventually foreclosed in a civil court action.

In March of 1862, Charles Ostner, a man destined to become a famous artist, arrived in Florence on snowshoes. He reported the miners were destitute and the government was sending provisions from Walla Walla. Ostner made a life-size statue of George Washington in front of Ben Anderson's saloon to celebrate the Fourth of July, 1863.[56] Later, he got lost near Buffalo Hump and wandered for 35 days. Three packers eventually found and saved him.[57]

John Krall was one of the interesting and successful men of early Idaho who got his start at Florence. His story tells a great deal about the potential of Florence gold. He was German-born, but went to England when young to learn the baking trade. He was too wild for such a life in his early days, and took off to see the world by ship. After many adventures, including nearly being the emergency rations for a starving crew, he jumped ship and headed to the American Northwest.

Krall owned a bakery at French Prairie, Washington Territory, and then went to Vancouver, presently in Washington State, where he had another bakery and lunch trade serving mainly the soldiers from Fort Vancouver. After Lincoln's election and the beginning of the Civil War, the post was abandoned and Krall's lucrative business went down hill. Krall and his partner knew they had to go elsewhere but lacked the capital to set up again. Krall told his credulous partner he could raise the money. He bought up all the calico cloth, beads, and mining supplies he could afford and set out. He went all the way into the future state of Idaho, across the Clearwater River and into the camp of Lawyer, one of the Nez Perce headmen.

Krall asked to see Lawyer and the Chief greeted him: "Hello, you bakery man Vancouver."[58] Krall explained in a 1912 interview that he always fed the Indians who came into Vancouver and he was sure they would remember him. He asked for quarters for the night, and in the morning opened his packs and showed his goods. The tribe had just received a government payment and had cash to spend. Krall

Figure. 2.14 Portraits of three husbands of Isabella and her sisters. This was in the
Boise Statesman article describing the reunion of the three Kelly sisters in 1911.

took in $775 in cash, more than $500 of which was profit. He got a passport from the chief to the next camp, a smaller one, where he sold the rest of the Calico and beads. Then he went on to Florence, which was at the beginning of the boom that forever gave it the description of "fabulous." There he sold his miners supplies. At Elk City, on the way to Florence, John grubstaked some men who then struck it rich at Florence. They gave him a claim in repayment.

The pay streak at this claim was just three feet below the surface and Krall's first rocker-load netted $25.25. He worked the claim all the winter of 1861. He took out $300 to $1,000 per day. When he thought the streak ran out he asked Three Finger Smith what he would give him for the claim. Smith said $1,000 and the deal was sealed. Smith went on to take out $75,000 in just three months before he left for the Weiser Valley several hundred miles to the south.[59] Krall went to Lewiston to finish out the winter of 1861-62 and opened a bakery. Bread sold for 50 cents a loaf, as all materials were very expensive. In the fall of 1862, Krall went south to the Boise Basin and settled briefly at Placerville. Smith, whose original name was Sylvester, once made the mistake of resting his hands on the end of the barrel of his muzzle-loading shotgun while he conversed with a friend. Sylvester's foot slid off its resting place on the fence and hit the hammer of the gun. His middle fingers on each hand were shot off, and he would never be known as Sylvester again. According to Smith's son Henry, Three-Finger recalled that residents of early Florence never turned their heads when they heard a shot for fear they'd get shot in the back.[60]

In June of 1862, Boone Helm shot and killed Dutch Fred.[61] Fred could whip anybody in town with his fists, but he was not a gunman. The men tangled once, but third parties disarmed them and left the weapons with a bartender. Helm apologized and left but then returned, seized his gun, and shot Fred in cold blood. The murderer escaped. Helm, a multiple murderer and a confessed cannibal, was eventually returned to Florence in the spring of 1863 for trial. According to Langford, a friend of Helm's bribed everyone involved and

Helm was found innocent. Helm was in Virginia City, Montana, in January, 1864 and hanged by the vigilantes the same night as Henry Plummer. He asked the vigilantes for a drink and they gave him a full tumbler from which he took a drink "as long as a telegraph pole."[62] The vigilantes were surprised that he wanted to meet his maker with whiskey on his breath. That would have been the least of his sins.

In his diary entry of 15 June 1862, P. W. Gillette wrote of Florence: "The Saloons are full of people. Many are gambling; hundreds drinking while some are simply idling away the time and listening to the alluring chink of some coin on the gaming tables which almost always culminate in shooting, and often killing. Not infrequently, some drunken ruffian draws his revolver and begins to shoot in the midst of the vast crowd, often killing or wounding someone and creating a fearful stampede. Such is Sunday in Florence."[63]

Gillette went on to add that, "Here the congressman, legislator, lawyer, merchant, farmer, laborer and sailor mingle in the same crowd, wear like slouch hats, blue shirts and ragged or patched breeches." Gillette's elegance as a wordsmith and his pessimistic view may have caused Florence to appear worse than it really was. He further added: "Nearly all the vast horde of gamblers, roughs and desperadoes are from California—the remainder, dregs and offspring of that foul collection of villains that flooded California in 1849 to 1852, 10 to 13 years ago. There is no law here, or none that sees, abates, retards or punishes crime."[64]

A letter to the Washington Statesman of Walla Walla in August 1862 described the public amusements in Florence. "In addition to cutting and shooting, which are practiced to a considerable extent, the various drinking saloons of Florence have musicians engaged, who nightly hold forth for the delectation of visitors. The incongruity of gaming while the music of the masters is being artistically performed is striking; illustrating the fact that the noblest and basest passions exist in the same men—heaven and hell conjoined." This report said there had been several concerts, and a Miss Rand and a Mr. Lindsay had sung very well at them.

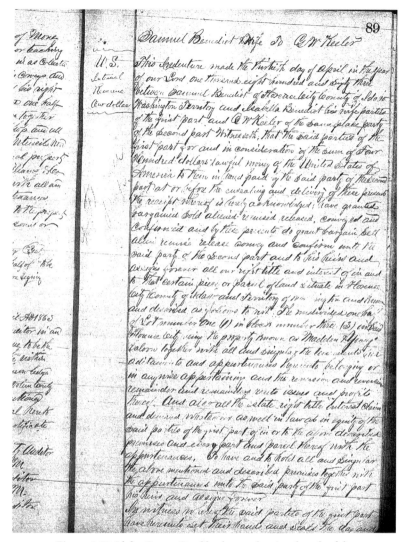

Figure. 2.15 Idaho County Deed book page showing the sale of the Benedict Saloon as Sam and Isabella left Florence.

The Fourth of July, 1862, at Florence was celebrated with a great dogfight. "Jack Heenan" of Yreka was facing "Danger" of San Francisco for the sum of $500 a side. Admission at the Miller's saloon was $1 to see all the action.[65] Miss Rand held another concert that evening.[66] Highbrow and lowbrow were both available in Florence. The Statesman had it right: Heaven and Hell were conjoined.

Later in September, 1862, there had been 1,318 mining claims filed on the record books in Florence. Some of these were actually located in the Elk City area.

By the end of 1862, efforts at law enforcement had increased, but there were ample reasons to agree with Gillette's position too. Among the early killings in the mining area were these: a Frenchman shot Robert Upcreek at Oro Fino in September of 1861; Mr. Hypolite, owner of a large pack train and $5,000 in gold, murdered on the road in October of 1861; Ned Meany killed in a quarrel at Jackson's ferry near Lewiston, November 1861; Two masked men entered a house in Lewiston in December, 1861, and carried away $500, after shooting fatally one of the inmates; Matt Bledsoe killed James Harman at Slate Creek, Salmon River in a quarrel over cards, December 1861; Four Murders were committed in Lewiston in August and September 1860; Savester Scott was killed in a gunfight at Florence in January 1862; Three murders in March 1862 at Florence, including the murder of Dutch Fred by Boone Helm; William Kiaby killed John Maples at Lewiston in July 1863; Mr. Winters killed Mr. Pierce in Florence in September 1862; and Morrissy, a desperado, was killed at Elk City about the same time.[67] In addition, "two colored men and a half-breed" had killed an Indian near Lewiston in late March of 1862.[68]

A man named McEwan paid an Indian he unjustly wounded $50 in settlement at Florence in late March of 1862.[69] The same newspaper reported that the whiskey famine in the town had been alleviated by the arrival of a new supply.

There was an election scheduled in Florence on July 14, 1862, but scarcely anyone knew of it or cared.[70] A constable, alcalde and justice of the peace were needed. In September, when the new jail was nearly finished, a man named Winters was being held for killing a Mr. Pierce, and the local thieves had all "skeedaddled" after viewing the jail construction with "melancholy jealousy."[71] Actually, the report in this case was exaggerated, not all the roughs had left.

The winter of 1862-63, it "snowed 113 days more or less in quick succession," according to Alonzo Brown's memory. His daughter skied over the roof of his house that winter. As many miners began to leave for the Boise Basin, hundreds of miles to the south, the 20 stores in Florence were in financial trouble. The largest one went broke. Brown had the second largest store and hung on for a while before moving to Warren. He sold his Florence store building for a mere $25 when he left.

On the Fourth of July, 1863, former Yreka resident Chas. A. Barnard was seriously injured firing a salute for the holiday.[72] By the middle of 1863, fabulous Florence was just plain Florence, it wasn't fabulous anymore. The town had a terminal illness, but would endure an exceedingly slow death. Thirty years later when new mines were opened, Florence revived for a few years and then took its good old time to finally die.

Isabella and Sam

Isabella was working in her father's Florence store when she first noticed the handsome Hollander, Samuel Benedict, the village blacksmith.[73] Adkison's account of the Benedict family said Isabella was content helping in her father's store until she met Samuel. They decided to elope due to her parent's objections. The young couple headed for Washington (Warrens), and were out in the deep snow when father Kelley overtook them. Adkison said the parents objected at first, but with her parent's blessings, Isabella married Samuel Benedict on 9 February 1863 in Florence with Methodist minister John Roger officiating.[74] The marriage must have irked the Irish Catholic Kelly family. In fact, they may not have considered the ceremony valid. Adkison's tale of parental consent does not seem to tell the whole story. The historical record tells more details. Isabella was 15 years, two months, five days old, and Sam was 27 years, 5 months and 20 days old. John Kelly was charged with assaulting Henry Burbage with a club on February 8, the day before his daughter's wedding. Kelly was fined $10 and costs. Was this an angry outburst over someone talking about the impending marriage or perhaps just a bad mood over the situation?

Soon after the wedding, Isabella's father, John Kelly, was not taking well to his new son-in-law, Benedict. John filed suit on the 24
March against Benedict to recover 300 pounds of flour, valued at
ninety dollars.[75] A week later, Mrs. John (Sarah) Kelly appeared in
court to represent her husband's claim. On March 31 the claim was
settled and the suit withdrawn. Another sign of conflict with John
Kelly quickly appeared. Samuel and his new wife filed suit against
John Kelley (sic), her father, to get the bride's clothing from him.[76]
A writ of Replevin was issued and her clothes were finally delivered.
On March 31, the parties appeared in court and gave notice of the
settlement, and the suit was withdrawn. Both court actions were
resolved the same day. John Kelly probably was not eager to see his
young daughter married. He may not have been pleased with the
choice of Mr. Benedict as a son-in-law, or needed Isabella's help
in the store, or wanted her to marry a Catholic. Whatever the case,
conflict was obvious.

On 8 May 1863, John Kelly was back in court for threatening to
kill his daughter and son-in-law. The court made him post a bond of
$1,000 to keep the peace, and in particular not to attack his daugh-
ter's family. John refused, and was remanded to the sheriff, but three
days later the bond was paid. Some of the money went to Sam and
Isabella as witness fees.

Sam and Isabella sold their interest in the Madden Saloon" in
Florence to G. W. Keeler for $400.[77] They were planning to leave
Florence.

In July, 1863, some citizens of Florence set up a committee to so-
licit donations for the sanitary fund for the relief of sick or wounded
soldiers of the Union or Federal army.[78] Among the many contributions was a $5 gift from Samuel Benedict. He was a Union man.

Isabella's younger brother, John James, recalled these days in a
newspaper article in 1916 when he returned from Staten Island to
see his boyhood haunts in Idaho.[79] He said he was left in Florence
with Isabella and her new husband, that he incorrectly identified as

Mr. Robie. He accompanied them on a wedding trip from Florence to Walla Walla, then through the fledgling town of Boise, on to Placerville and other Boise Basin towns, and then returned to Florence. This would indicate that the friction between Isabella and her husband with her father had eased enough that they wanted to visit at the new Kelly home. John Kelly's family had apparently moved to Boise Basin by this time.

(Freedom), Slate Creek, Idaho

Charles Silverman, one of the first to have a claim at Elk City, apparently had an agreement with a Nez Perce chief named Whistle Knocker to allow him to put in a station at the point where the trail left the Salmon River to head up the mountains. In the spring of 1862, John Wood paid $1,000 to Silverman to take over the spot. Wood planted apple trees and was a member of the first Territorial Legislature that met at Lewiston. By 1870, a post office was established, and in 1874 the Wood family sold some of their holdings to their son-in-law, Charles F. Cone, who opened his own way station and ranched.

Early in 1864, Sam and Isabella Benedict moved down the mountain to the town of Freedom, eventually renamed Slate Creek, at the Mouth of Slate Creek where it meets the Salmon River (River of No Return). Both Sam and Isabella were northerners, and Freedom was a Union town in a world where the Civil War commanded violent loyalties.

Figure. 2.16 Slate Creek sign in the center of the village of Slate Creek by the bridge. Photo by the author.

The legality of the settlement was in question until Congress ratified the 1863 treaty. It was technically still Nez Perce land. This was the site at which the earliest trail to Florence left the Salmon River to go up the steep trail to the gold camp. Adkison said the Benedicts went to Freedom (Slate Creek) because it was a Union rather than Con-

*Figure. 2.17 View from the center of Slate Creek showing the surrounding area.
Photo by the author.*

federate camp. Also, several pack trains had wintered there and the stock needed shoeing. Samuel was assured of work in his profession.

Their first son, Grant, was born at Freedom, at the mouth of Slate Creek, on 9 October 1864.[80] The full name of the first White child born in Idaho County was Ulysses Samuel Grant Benedict—the Civil War was still raging in the East and General Grant had become the leader of the Union forces.[81] The general had a namesake in far off Idaho.

End Notes

[1] William A. Olson file. Special Collections, University of Idaho Library.
J. Loyal Adkison, "Benedict Family Closely Related to Early Idaho County History," Idaho County Free Press, Grangeville, Idaho, 27 March 1952. This was an obituary for Grant Benedict as well as a history of the family. Some sources list her birth year as 1848.

[2] Elizabeth's name came from Idaho County Marriage Records.

[3] Unsourced obituaries in family scrapbook. She was born in 20 December 1851. She must have been more of a foster child with the Kelly family than a friend of Sarah's.

[4] Thompson & West, *History of Yuba County California*, 1879, Chapter xxxix, n.p.

[5] Edward Lansing Wells, "Notes on the Winter of 1861-1862 in the Pacific Northwest," *Northwest Science*, vol. xxi, p.p. 76-83.

[6] Edward Lansing Wells, "Notes on the Winter of 1861-1862 in the Pacific Northwest," *Northwest Science*, vol. xxi, p. 81.

[7] "Fabulous Florence," *Idaho Yesterdays*, Summer 1962, p. 22.

[8] Kathryn L. McKay, "Gold for the Taking: Historical Overview of the Florence Mining District, Idaho County, Idaho," Nez Perce National Forest report, 1998, p. 261.

[9] *Yreka Semi-Weekly Journal*, Yreka, California, 9 April 1862, p. 1, c. 2-5.

[10] *Yreka Journal*, Yreka, CA., 2 April 1862, p. 2, c. 2.

[11] These songs have been recorded by Idaho music historian Gary Eller.

[12] *Yreka Semi-Weekly Journal*, 28 May 1862, p. 2, c. 2.

[13] *Yreka Semi-Weekly Journal*, 23 August 1862, p. 1, c. 3-4.

[14] *Yreka Semi-Weekly Journal*, 3 May 1862, p. 4, c. 1.

[15] *Yreka Semi-Weekly Journal*, 2 July 1862, p. 4, c. 2.

[16] *Yreka Semi-Weekly Journal*, 8 October 1862, p. 3, c. 2.

[17] Jones, J. Roy. *Saddle Bags in Siskiyou*. c. 1953, Reprinted Happy Camp, CA: Naturegraph Publishers, 1980. p. 101.

[18] *Yreka Semi-Weekly Journal*, 22 November 1862, p.1, c.

[19] *Yreka Semi-Weekly Journal*, 17 May 1862, p. 2, c. 6.

[20] *Idaho Daily Statesman*, 17 December 1911, Section II, p. 3. c. 1-2.

[21] *Idaho Daily Statesman*, 17 December 1911, Section II, p. 3, c. 1-2.

[22] Ruth and Mike Dakis, "Guilty or not guilty? Vigilantes on Trial," *Idaho Yesterdays*, winter 1968-69, p. 2.

[23] Kathryn L. McKay, *Gold for the Taking*, p. 364.

[24] Idaho county Deed book I, p. 39.

[25] Herman Reinhart, *The Golden Frontier*, p. 223.

[26] No mention of Elizabeth Castello being at the dance is found in any source.

[27] Herman Reinhart remembered these nicknames, but he also remembered the shootout occurring at the dance.

[28] Robbins was a member of the first Grand Jury ever called in the future Idaho in 1861, and was still enforcing the law 45 years later. *Idaho Daily Statesman*, 8 January 1905, p. 4, c. 1.

[29] January 1, 1863 was a Thursday.

[30] Langford, *Vigilante Days and Ways*, p. 46. Langford said the fight occurred two days after the ball.

[31] *Morning Oregonian*, Portland, 20 January 1863, p. 2, c. 1.

[32] Langford, *Vigilante Days and Ways*, p. 46.

[33] Byron Defenbach, *Idaho the Place and Its People*, Vol. I, 1933, p. 327.

[34] McConnell, *Early History of Idaho*, p. 66.

[35] The Talbot grave was rediscovered and is now one of the few positively identified with a marker at the Florence cemetery on National Forest land.

[36] *Morning Oregonian*, Portland, 20 January 1863, p. 2, c. 1. This version is very close to that McConnell and Langford told years later. See also *Washington Statesman*, Walla Walla, 17 January 1863, p. 2, c. 4. It took just over two weeks for the news to reach Walla Walla from Florence in the dead of winter.

[37] *The Weekly Capital*, Boise, Idaho, 24 February 1900, p. 6, c. 1-2.

[38] Federal Writer's Project, *Idaho, A Guide in Word and Picture*, New York: Oxford University Press, 1937, p. 14.

[39] *Washington Statesman*, Walla Walla, 17 January 1863, p. 2, c. 4. Their report was 14 balls in "Willoby" and Talbotte five.

[40] Hawley, *History of Idaho*, Vol. I, p. 128.

[41] Elsensohn, *Pioneer Days in Idaho County*, Vol. I, p. 59. Witnesses called included William Courtney, Barney Roark, Benjamin Davis, George Ranning, John Moorehead, Sheriff Keenan, J. B. Dunlap, Mitchell Caldwell, J. H. Curley, J. B. Oldham, and James Graham. Oldham had been in the fire department in Yreka, California, in 1859 along with J. D. Williams. See *History of Siskiyou County, California, Illustrated with Views of Residences, Business Buildings and Natural Scenery, and Containing Portraits and Biographies of Its Leading Citizens and Pioneers*. Oakland, CA: D. J. Stewart & Co., 1881, p. 188.

[42] *Morning Oregonian*, Portland, Oregon, 21 January 1863, p. 2, c. 1.

[43] William B. Secrest, *Lawmen and Desperadoes*, p. 290. Barney Owsley. "Reminiscences," Idaho State University, Pocatello. Robert Bailey, *River of No Return*, 1935, p. 93. Owsley was 14 to 15 when the events occurred and nearly 90 when he related them.

[44] Byron Defenbach, *Idaho, the Place and Its People*, Vol. I, 1933, p. 328.

[45] Photocopy of the Idaho County Recorder's record book, p. 9. Olsen Collection, #393 Manuscript Group, University of Idaho Library, Special Collections.

[46] Brown was another Yreka man. He had declared bankruptcy there and was later famous for his involvement in the temperance movement in Idaho. See *Yreka Weekly Journal*, 24 Oct. 1861, p. 3, c. 5.

[47] Barbara Hegne, *Virginia City: Rascals & Renegades Plus a Few Forgotten People of the Comstock Lode.* Sparks, Nevada: published by the author, 2000, pp. 1-4.

[48] William J. McConnell (Captain of the Payette Vigilantes) and James S. Reynolds (Member of the Boise City Vigilantes) *Idaho's Vigilantes*, edited by Joyce Lindstrom, Moscow: University of Idaho Press, pp. 4-5. This version apparently originated years later with Major Fenn.

[49] Langford, *Vigilante Days and Ways.*

[50] There is a brief mention of this event in *Yreka Weekly Journal*, 4 March 1863, p. 2, c. 1.

[51] *Idaho Daily Statesman*, 1 May 1910, Section II, p. 5, c. 1-2.

[52] *Idaho Daily Statesman*, 3 Oct 1909, p. 6, c. 3 and 10 Oct 1909, p. 6, c. 3.

[53] "Autobiography of Alonzo F. Brown," *Echoes of the Past.* Vol. 1, no. 2, August 2002, pp. 8-15.

[54] Ronald H. Limbaugh, "Attitudes of the Population of Idaho Toward Law and Order, 1860-1870." p. 29.

[55] George Hendricks, *The Bad Men of the West*, p. 194. One Last Drink in the Hangman's Building," internet. http://www.virginiacity.com/sch05.htm.

[56] *Idaho Daily Statesman,* 13 December 1908, Section II, p. 7, c. 3 & 4.

[57] *Idaho Daily Statesman*, 1 May 1910, Section II, p. 5, c. 1-2.

[58] *Idaho Statesman*, Boise, Idaho, 1 December 1912, Section. II, p. 11, c. 5-6.

[59] *Idaho Statesman*, 1 December 1912, Section. II, p. 11, c. 5-6.

[60] Elsensohn, *Pioneer Days in Idaho County*, vol. I, p. 56.

[61] Haberman, Mike. "Vanishing Florence: An Early Idaho mining Metropolis Disappears into History," *Lewiston Morning Tribune*, 2 August 1998, Section. D. p. 1.

[62] *Washington Statesman*, Walla Walla, Washington, 2 August 1862, p. 2, c. 3.

[63] Haberman, Mike. "Vanishing Florence: An Early Idaho Mining Metropolis Disappears into History," *Lewiston Morning Tribune,* 2 August 1998, Section. D. p. 1.

[64] *Washington Statesman*, Walla Walla, Washington, 2 August 1862, p. 2, c. 3.

[65] *Yreka Semi-Weekly Journal*, Yreka, California, 16 July 1862, p. 2, c. 2.

[66] *Washington Statesman*, Walla Walla, Washington, 12 July 1862, p. 3, c. 2.

[67] *The Weekly Capital*, Boise, Idaho, 24 February 1900, p. 6, c. 1-2.

[68] *Washington Statesman*, Walla Walla, Washington, 5 April 1862, p. 2, c. 2.

[69] *Washington Statesman*, Walla Walla, Washington, 12 April 1862, p. 2, c. 4.

[70] *Washington Statesman*, Walla Walla, Washington, 12 July 1862, p. 3, c. 2.

[71] *Washington Statesman*, Walla Walla, Washington, 13 September 1862, p. 2, c. 3.

[72] *Yreka Semi-Weekly Journal*, Yreka, California, 25 July 1863, p. 2, c. 5.

[73] Adkison, J. Loyal. "Benedict Family Closely Related to Early Idaho History," *Idaho County Free Press*, Grangeville, Idaho, 27 March 1952.

[74] Idaho County marriage records. Some say they were the first couple married in "Idaho," but it was not yet Idaho Territory, only Idaho County of Washington Territory.

[75] Olson records U of I Special collections, p. 3 of papers on Benedict.

[76] Docket Book, Florence, Idaho, p. 54. Olsen Manuscript Collection, U of Idaho Special Collections.

[77] Idaho County Deed Book, number 1, page 89.

[78] *The Golden Age*, Lewiston, Idaho, Vol. 2, no. 2, 8 August 1863.

[79] "Visits Boise for First Time in 47 Years; Remembers How Old Fort Looked," *Idaho Statesman*, 8 Oct 1916.

[80] Kathryn L. McKay, *Gold for the Taking: Historical Overview of the Florence Mining District, Idaho County, Idaho*. United States Department of Agriculture, Nez Perce National Forest, Grangeville, Idaho, 1998, p. 243. This town was later known as Slate Creek.

[81] Adkison, J. Loyal. "Benedict Family Closely Related to Early Idaho History," *Idaho County Free Press*, 27 March 1952.

3

LIFE AT FREEDOM & WHITE BIRD

1865-30 April 1877

IN DECEMBER 1861, while the mouth of Slate Creek area was a place where goods destined for Florence were stored in tents, Matt Bledsoe killed James Harmon over a card game. The first district court was held in Florence in December of 1861 to handle this and other matters.[1] The most famous killings at Slate Creek started on April 28, 1862 when Jim "Brocky" Winters killed John Daly over a card game with a shot to the heart.[2] Brocky went to Florence where he killed James Pierce about four months later. Late in December that year, Brocky was back in Slate Creek. He went after Arthur (Ad) Chapman with a knife and Chapman defended himself successfully with an ax. Killing Brocky made Chapman a noteworthy name in the area. He would be remembered for much more.

After Ulysses Samuel Grant Benedict, the first Euro-American child born in Idaho County, joined the family in their log cabin in 1864, on 10 September 1866, Mary Caroline Benedict was born. Some sources list her birthplace as Lewiston, Idaho, which is not far away by boat, but a rough trip overland. Family collective memory believes Samuel had a blacksmith shop in Lewiston at the time of her birth. The family may have temporarily left Slate Creek. On October 9, 1868, Frances was born. In the Spring of 1871, a daughter, Nettie, was born, and Adelaide, born 4 November 1875, completed the family.

An advertisement in the Lewiston newspaper, July 4, 1867, touted John Wood's Slate Creek business:

"Slate Creek House, at the foot of Florence Mountain on Salmon River, Idaho county, John Wood proprietor. This is the house for miners en rout for Florence and Warren's mines early in the spring, and supplied with good beds, good food, prepared to please the appetite of the most dainty epicures, as well as the hardy miner."[3]

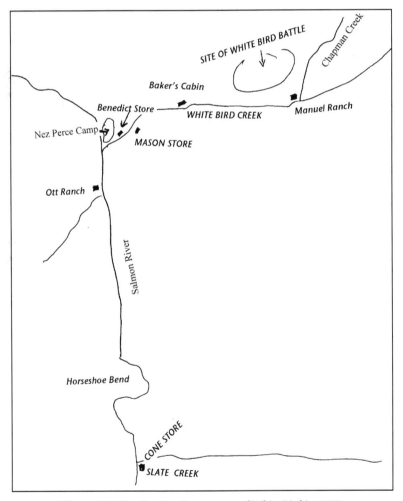

Figure. 3.1 Map showing the area around White Bird in 1877.

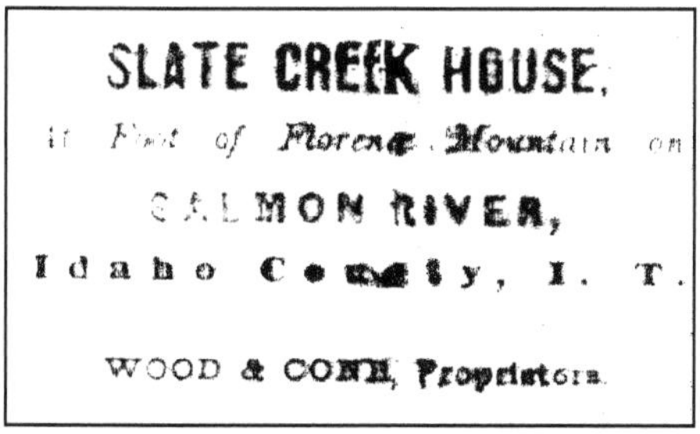

SLATE CREEK HOUSE,

i: F...t of *Florence Mountain* on

S.LMON RIVER,

I d a h o C o u n t y , I . T .

WOOD & CONE, Proprietors.

Figure. 3.2 Newspaper advertisement for Slate Creek House owned by Wood and Cone. 1867.

On 12 January 1868, Isabella's sister Sarah Kelly married Leander Dougherty in Boise County far to the south of Slate Creek. William J. Wakefield, who became well known in early Idaho, was one of the witnesses.[4] Dougherty had enlisted in the Civil War on 24 February 1864 at Oroville, California, and was mustered out on 14 May 1866, at San Francisco. He was in the California 1st Cavalry, Company A and went in a private, and out a sergeant.[5]

Isabella's sister, Sarah, later married her second husband, George Cartwright. They moved to the road between Boise and the Boise Basin. "The George Cartwrights developed a fine home and stock business on Shafer Creek and were known far and wide for their hospitality."[6]

Benedict paid $300 to Charles Snyder for the site where his store would stand near the confluence of White Bird Creek and the Salmon River a few miles down the Salmon from Slate Creek. The family began accumulating a considerable hold-

Figure 3.3 Portrait of Alex Orchard, husband of Mary Ann Kelly Orchard, and brother- in-law to Isabella. Photo from the collection of Deborah Starr.

ing after moving there. One source on Idaho history said there was a small influx of settlers to the Salmon River Valley in 1870 and one of those was Sam Benedict.

John M. Kelly

After his relocation, Isabella's father, John Kelly was joined by his two unmarried daughters at Boise Basin in 1864.[7] Over 50 years later, daughter Sarah remembered the tedious ride from Uma-

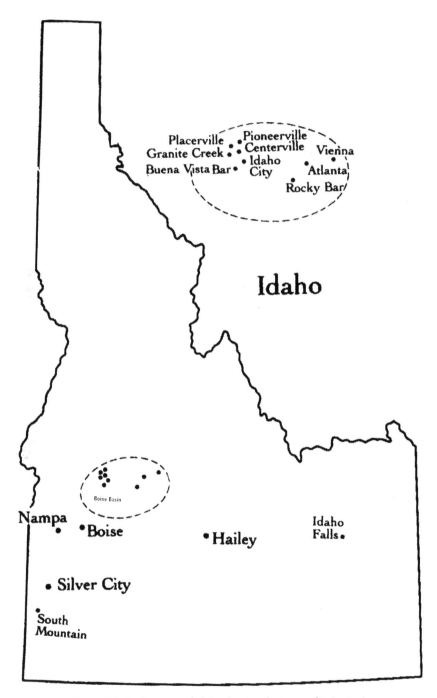

Figure. 3.4 Outline map of Idaho showing the towns of Boise Basin.

tilla (on the Columbia River in Oregon) to the Boise Basin. Mary Ann was married at Placerville in 1867. John planned an elaborated wedding, but Mary Ann and Mr. Alex Orchard "stole a march upon the family and were quietly married at the home a friend." They lived

Figure. 3.5 Placerville, Idaho, welcome sign. Mary Ann and Alex Orchard lived here for several years. Photo by the author.

at Placerville several years and then went to Idaho City to run the Orchard Hotel for many more years.

Orchard was born in Shannon County, Missouri in 1836.[8] He went to California in 1850 or 1851 and then went to Auburn, Oregon. When the gold Rush to Florence started he was one of the first there. In the summer of 1862, news of the gold strike in Boise Ba-

Figure. 3.6. Placerville Idaho, cemetery sign. John Kelly is buried here. Photo by the author.

sin reached Florence, and Orchard went south with the noted Standifer party of prospectors. This group was one of the first to arrive at the new gold camp. After their marriage, Mr. and Mrs. Orchard stayed in Placerville some years. After they moved to Idaho City, the County Seat, Orchard was elected County Assessor. After three terms in that position Alex and Mary Ann ran their hotel.

In October of 1868, less than a week after the birth of grandchild Frances back on the Salmon River, John Kelly got into an altercation at Granite Creek, where he ran a public house, with a butcher named Perkins regarding some hogs. Kelly had sold the hogs to a third party

Figure. 3.7 Headstone of John Kelly, Isabella's father. Photo from the collection of Deborah Starr.

who in turn sold then to Perkins. Kelly was dissatisfied with the sale and wanted the hogs back, and thus began the altercation. Between 9 and 10 in the morning, they shot it out. A stage driver on Pinkham's stage reached Idaho City that day with the news that the wounds of both parties were superficial. It was only his reporting that was superficial. Kelly was shot through the body and Perkins shot in the groin. The attending physician thought both would die.[9] The Boise newspaper reprinted this a few days later but had additional details by then.[10] The hogs really belonged to Perkins, according to them, and Kelly wanted a fuss with Perkins. The affair happened at the slaughter house. Kelly lingered 47

Figure 3.8 John Kelly's plot in Placerville. Photo from the collection of Deborah Starr.

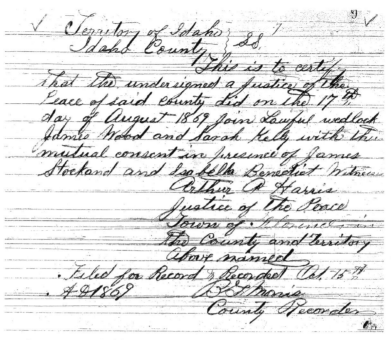

Figure 3.9 Record of the marriage of Sarah Kelly and James Wood at Florence. Isabella was one of the witnesses at her mother's second marriage.

hours before passing. Dr. Wagoner then left to attend to Perkins. The next day, the Idaho City newspaper, then in a bitter rivalry with the Boise paper, said Kelly shot first and the ball hit the tip of Perkins hip, lodged in his flesh, and prostrated him.[11] He then got up—or some witnesses said a third party was responsible—and fired at Kelly. The ball went through his neck.

John Kelly was described as a "pioneer of Granite Creek, a man of warm impulses, very set in his opinions, a devoted friend and open in his dealings. He was buried on Monday and his funeral was largely attended. He leaves a wife in Granite Creek, and his two married daughters are living there."[12] Isabella probably learned of these events a few days after they happened. In November that year, the Kelly estate was $49.52 delinquent in property tax on "Kelly's Hall" in Granite Creek.[13] John Kelly fought, threatened and assaulted through out his life, but he also fed his family and supported a foster child. No simplistic evaluation can cover his life.

Figure 3.10 Classical portrait of Sarah, Isabella's mother.
Photo from the Deb Starr collection.

On 17 August 1869, Isabella's mother, Sarah Kelly, married James Wood, brother of innkeeper John Wood, at Florence, with Isabella being one of the witnesses.[14] She had come north to be with her oldest daughter and had left her little son with his sister Mary Ann. The Wood family would be intertwined with Isabella's for years to come.

The Tragic Lynching of James Wood

Isabella's step-father James Wood suffered a tragic death that impacted the entire family, and speaks to the law and order situation in Idaho at the time. The *Oregonian* newspaper of Portland reported that on January 18, 1870 the telegraph informed them of a tragedy in Lewiston—the lynching of James Wood. They opined that James Wood was hung as a result of the commutation of his sentence. They said there was a strong feeling against Wood by the citizens of Lewiston and the hanging was probably done "after the style of a vigilance committee."[15] They mentioned that his brother, a citizen of Oregon, had gone to Boise to get the commutation and had expressed fear that something like this might happen.[16]

Wood's brother, the Reverend T. A. Wood wrote a long letter to the Boise Statesman explaining his side of the events.[17]

> With your permission, I will give the circumstances connected with the killing of one Thos. Duffy, and the mobbing of J. M. Wood, and the reasons that have forced me to believe J. M. Wood innocent of the unlawful killing of Thos. Duffy.
>
> It has ever been a matter patent to my mind, that when any man or set of men have had unjust cause, that fact will be seen in the manner of their defense. In this case, most, if not all, the reports in circulation against Wood were totally false—not a word of their truth is to be found in the evidence. One other point in this connection: lying was not the only weapon used, but threats of personal injury was made by the prosecution against any witness who would testify to any facts

for Wood. Most, if not all, the witnesses for Wood were thus threatened, as may be seen in written testimony. Some three of the witnesses for the defense were driven off by this same mob, while others appealed to the court for protection.

J. W. Eaton was first employed by Wood to defend him. He misled the friends of Wood by his letters, and thereby prevented them coming to his aid; he robbed Wood of the money sent to him by his father, and did not make one single move in his favor, but by his demeanor before the public prejudiced his cause rather than helped him. He is a low, drunken sot, and is a disgrace to the profession. On the day set for trial, Eaton was dismissed and Hon. A. Leland employed. Leland said to me, "I had no time to prepare his cause, and never having had a case of this kind, I was wholly incompetent to do him justice; but had I had someone to assist me, we could have easily cleared him." This much I can say, Leland did well considering his opportunity. He was threatened too by the same band of gamblers and roughs. The witnesses, who had decamped, could not be induced to return for fear; and without money to induce them to return (as they were beyond the authority of the court) or power to offer protection to those who remained, he lost much material testimony, and yet enough was driven to provide his innocence.

As to the relative character of the two men, in testimony, it appeared thus: J. M. Wood, it was proven, did not drink, gamble, or use profane language, and he was peaceable and so reputed till this occurrence, a small man, his weight was 140 pounds. It is in proof, that Thos. Duffy was a dangerous man—large man—constant drinker, etc.; and that he had in California killed one man, had on one occasion entered at "high 12", the house of Frank Creely and beat a Frenchman on Camas Prairie near to death. A revolver was seen, and Wood was knowing to all this, and of course suspected the same treatment when attacked. Duffy had threatened to take Wood's life times without number, as proven, had they admitted the testimony, that Duffy, not three hours before the affray, whipped his woman (not wife) because she hid his revolver to keep him from killing Wood. Evidence for the defense show that the evening before Duffy said, "If you don't leave this town I will kill you." Similar testimony is given as to other times. It was not in the evidence that Wood had ever harmed Duffy, or that he had quarreled with him.

As to the actual killing, I will give you substance, what I find in testimony before me; Wood was sitting on the corner or a table in a saloon one foot under him, face from the door, head resting on elbow on table, watching a game of cards, when Duffy came into the house, accompanied by two men known to Wood as his enemies, making the three that he had been informed were looking for him. Lewis Domingus testified: "Duffy approached Wood with foul words, in a striking attitude. Duffy's movements caused me to get out of the way." This witness was already at quite a distance from them. Other testimony says Duffy struck two blows before Wood got off the table. One witness for prosecution says Duffy put his hand upon Wood; one said he heard a blow others heard him use loud words. Duffy's ante-post mortem statement is sufficient of itself. He said, "I believe I struck at Wood first." There was not a witness could or would say they heard a noise—did not know what caused it, called their attention, and when they looked around they saw Wood in the act of getting off the table or drawing a knife. Duffy said to a man just after the affray, when asked who was to be blamed, "Kitty is to be blamed for all this." He never, as I have been creditably informed, blamed Wood for what he did.

As to this commutation by the Governor of Idaho. The testimony, as taken down by the Court, and two affidavits were ... error to pardon him, as they said they saw nothing in the evidence of his guilt. If the governor is to be blamed for anything it is not for pardoning him at once.

As to his being mobbed. If I should say, that the same parties who sought to intimidate Wood's witnesses and forged those falsehoods to create a public opinion, were the low, ill-bred canines that broke into the jail, dragged him out and hung him, some would think I was far out of the way.

The good citizens of Lewiston took no part in this disgraceful tragedy, but men of the baser sort have done the work that will forever haunt them.

In conclusion, it would be proper to say, that I have read all the testimony and am ready to prove every assertion herein made to be true as stated. If he had kept a squaw, a saloon or even spent all his money at the bar, those who mobbed him would not have done it. Such is my honest belief induced by evidence in my possession. Of course, those whose criminality causes them to spend hours "ill at ease" will seek to refute the above but to such I will say, we will see you again."

T. A. Wood

On January 1, 1870, Territorial Governor Ballad issued a commutation of the death sentence imposed on James Wood from execution to life in prison.[18] Sheriff John G. Berry, Nez Perce County, wrote a letter to governor Ballard of Idaho Territory that on January 13, 1870, armed, masked persons forcibly entered the jail at Lewiston and removed the prisoner and hanged him until he was dead.[19] Isabella's mother Sarah was a widow for the second time.

After the shooting and the lynching, Mrs. John Kelly Wood decided to return to New York State where she had relatives, and had lived before. Ten year-old John James Kelly was a reluctant traveler with his mother. He hid several times on the trip and slowed them up. Forty-eight years later he remembered this all well.

The People of the United States of the Territory of Idaho,

against

James M. Wood Defendant,

To the Sheriff of Nez Perce Co. I.T.

Greeting

Whereas application having been made to me, to commute the sentence of Death under which said James M. Wood now rests, for the crime of murder, in the Killing of one Thomas J. Duffy, in the County of Nez Perce, in the Territory of Idaho on or about the fourth day of July A.D. 1869. and it appearing to me from the papers on file in the Office of the Secretary of Idaho containing the statement of the trial, evidence &c, and after a full and careful examination of the files in said case, and from the authenticated statements and petitions therein of many good and reliable citizens of the County wherein said homicide occurred, that there is good and sufficient reason for the exercise of executive clemency.

Now Therefore by virtue of the power in me, by the law vested, in such cases, I do hereby declare that the sentence of death by hanging, pronounced by the District Court of the first Judicial District in the.

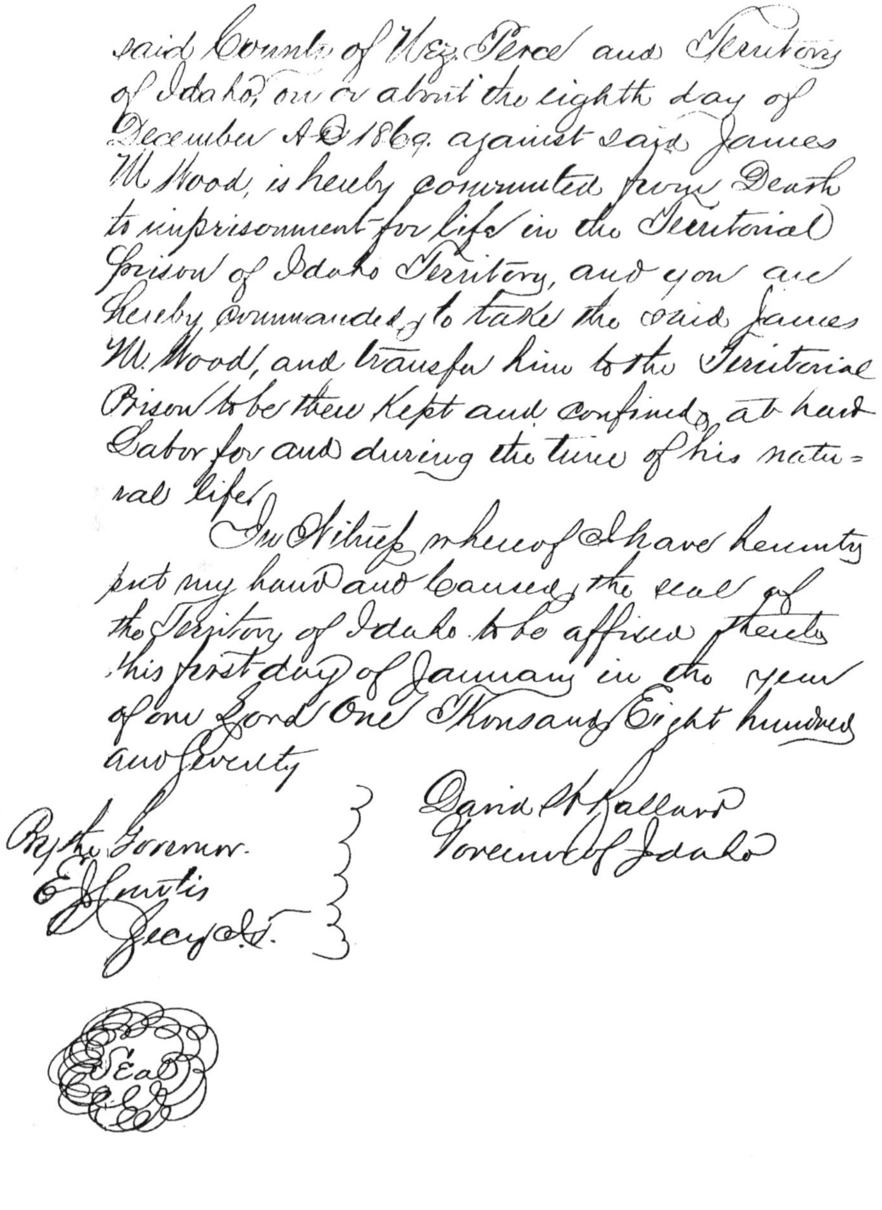

said County of Nez Perce and Territory
of Idaho, on or about the eighth day of
December AD 1869. against said James
M. Wood, is hereby commuted from Death
to imprisonment for life in the Territorial
Prison of Idaho Territory, and you are
hereby commanded to take the said James
M. Wood, and transfer him to the Territorial
Prison to be there kept and confined, at hard
Labor for and during the time of his natu-
ral life.

In Witness whereof I have hereunto
put my hand and caused the seal of
the Territory of Idaho to be affixed thereto
this first day of January in the year
of our Lord One Thousand Eight hundred
and Seventy

David H. Ballard
Governor of Idaho

By the Governor.
E. J. Curtis
Secy of I.

Figure. 3.11. Document sent to Nez Perce County sheriff from the
governor commuting the death sentence of James Wood.
Photocopy from the collection of Deborah Starr.

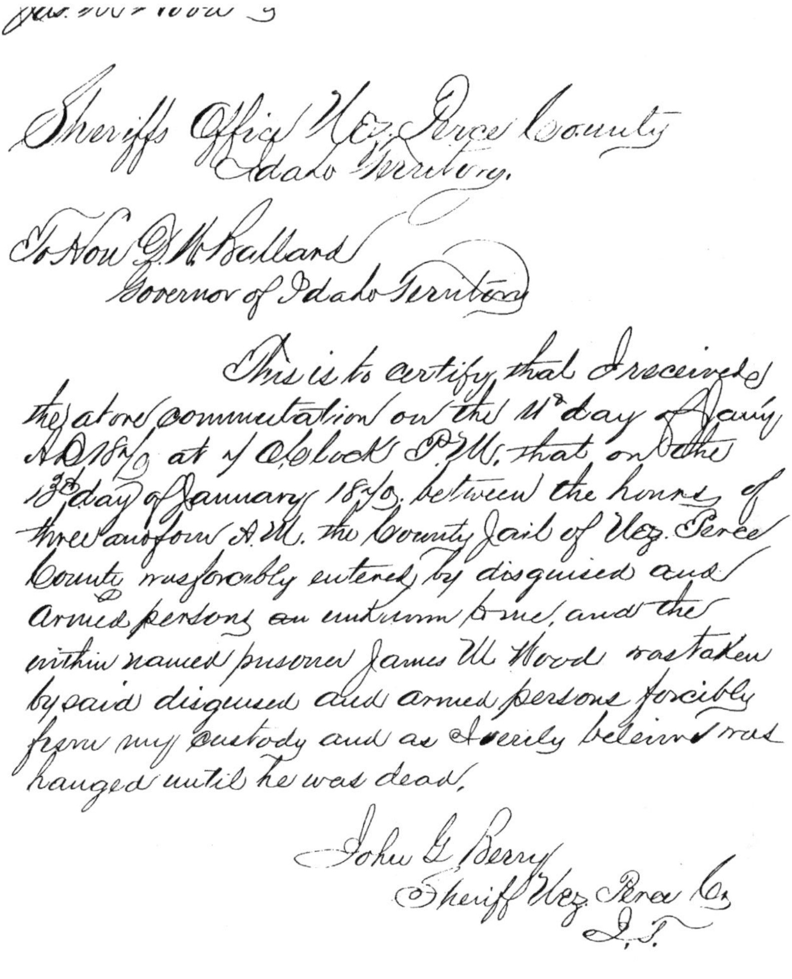

Sheriffs Office Nez Perce County
Idaho Territory.

To Hon D. W. Ballard
Governor of Idaho Territory

This is to certify that I received the above commutation on the 11th day of Jany A.D. 1870 at 7 O'clock P.M. that on the 13th day of January 1870, between the hours of three and four A.M. the County Jail of Nez Perce County was forcibly entered by disguised and armed persons an unknown to me, and the within named prisoner James W. Wood was taken by said disguised and armed persons forcibly from my custody and as I verily believe was hanged until he was dead.

John G. Berry
Sheriff Nez Perce Co
I. T.

Figure. 3.12. Sheriff Berry's letter to Idaho Governor Ballard explaining the lynching of James Wood. Photocopy from the collection of Deborah Starr.

The Benedict Store on Salmon River

In August 1869, Samuel Benedict filed suit against his wife Isabella and her mother Sarah Kelly for return of his goods and chattels valued at \$100.[20] The women allegedly had taken a feather bed, a pair of blankets, three pillows, a gold watch and chain, a finger ring, a pair of earrings, gold scales and other articles on the 8th of May 1869 without the plaintiff's consent. He had demanded return and they

Figure. 3.13 Photo of the Benedict store at the confluence of Whitebird Creek and the Salmon River. The store was on the lower right. This shows why the only practical egress was across the creek or downstream. Climbing this magnificent butte was not practical. The store and home were burned during the war of 1877.

had refused. The day before the action was to be heard in court, Samuel Benedict appeared and withdrew the suit. This sounds like a trial separation that was finally resolved. It was certainly an embarrassment to have such private information in the public record. One has to wonder if these events influenced Isabella's perception or testimony about her husband's later involvement with the Nez Perce

Figure. 3.14 Whitebird Creek in front of the Benedict home site. The brush was probably thicker then and the creek was low when this photo was taken in late October. The flow is generally much greater in June. Photo by the author.

and the start of the 1877 War. Perhaps it was just the standard mother-in-law problem.

In November of 1869, Margaret Popham, Jeanette Manuel's mother died of bowel cancer. The Pophams were living in the area and Margaret was buried at Slate Creek.

At White Bird, Sam Benedict's family was enumerated in the 1870 U. S. Census. Inexplicably, Isabella was listed as Jane and oldest son Grant was listed as Geo. Cassie (Mary) was 5, Flora (Frances) 3, and Sam was a blacksmith. Perhaps the Census recorder was hearing impaired.

In the spring of 1871, a daughter, Nettie, was born. A brief mention of her death in September of 1873 remains about the only information regarding her brief life. Also in 1871, the first Euro-American settlers arrived in the Wallowa Valley of Oregon to compete with the band of Nez Perce that had called it home for millennia. Seemingly, this would have no effect

Figure 3.15 A 1936 photo by Mark Taylor shows that the old Benedict cellar, cut into the bluff, was still intact. Photo from the collection of Deborah Starr.

on the Benedict family but it indeed would. The stage was set for conflict, and this event too would lead to grief.

Isabella's old friend, Jeanette Manuel, had married Williams in Florence shortly after Isabella was married in early 1863, but later that year, November 1863, he was killed in Idaho City. After returning to her parents' home, which was no longer in Florence but had moved to Warren, she next married John J. "Jack or J. J." Manuel in Warren. Eventually, the Manuel family moved to a ranch near the confluence of Chapman and White Bird Creeks, upstream from the town of Whitebird, and upstream from the Benedict store. Arthur "Ad" Chapman sold the homestead to them on 23 September

Figure. 3.16 On the left Whitebird Creek enters the River of No Return. Photo by author, October 2011.

Figure. 3.17 Benedict home and store site, Oct. 2011. Photo by the author.

1873 for $1,500. The two belles of fabulous Florence again lived close to each other, but now they were both mothers, not young teenagers.

When the Benedict children were old enough to go to school, Samuel built a school across the creek from their home. The first teacher was Frances Aram, who later became Mrs. Henry Johnson.

An inventory of the building and accouterments was made years later as part of the Benedict claim filed for compensation for losses suffered in the Indian War.[21] They had a one-and-a-half story frame dwelling, a frame store 12 by 28, a large frame barn, a small frame schoolhouse, and a frame, dirt-floored blacksmith shop. There was a milk house made of stone with walls four-foot thick and built with one end and part of the two adjacent sides into the bank. They had

Figure. 3.18 View to the south from the Benedict home site. Photo by the author.

200 fruit trees, including apples, pears, plums, peaches and cherries. They also had grape vines and other small fruit. They had in addition, 106 head of cattle, 20 horses, 8 hogs, and

50 chickens. They were prospering.

A newspaper reporter, only by-lined as Fadden, went through this area in the late spring of 1874 and described all the settlers he encountered. Fadden described neigh- bor James Baker's place

Figure. 3.19 *View to the east of the Benedict home site. Photo by the author.*

as very fine and painted white. Baker told him, "If I had a wife I'd be the happiest man in Idaho, by god, sir."[22] Lower down the creek, at Benedict's place: "He (Benedict) is improving his place all in his power; says it's the best place in the world. He keeps a house for the accommodation of travelers, …"[23]

"On White Bird Jack Manuel is flourishing like a green bay tree, and is making the wilderness blossom like a tulip bed. He has

brought in a ditch for irrigating purposes and is now independent of rain. As one of our earliest pioneers, Jack has many friends. All wish him success and hope that now, 'under his own vine and fig tree' he will prosper as he deserves." In September of that year, 2-year-old Nettie Benedict died, casting a pall over the prosperity of the family and the whole area.

The first council between settlers and the Wallowa Band of Nez Perce Indians was held

Figure. 3.20 *The ancient trees on the Benedict site. Photo by the author.*

Figure. 3.21 The business at the Benedict site as of October 2011. Photo by the author.

in 1872 to try to resolve differences. In late spring of 1873, the Modoc Indian War in California was credited by the White settlers of Idaho with arousing old feelings of revenge in the Nez Perce. Supposedly, the Idaho Native Americans were neglecting their crops and riding through the country that year attending councils as never before. President Grant signed an executive order granting half the Wallowa Valley to the Nez Perce in hopes of solving the problem. The settler's response in the Idaho County area all around White Bird was to organize defense companies in case conflict with Native Americans began.

In March of 1874, Larry Ott, who lived at Horse Shoe Bend on the Salmon River, near to the Benedict ranch, shot and killed "an Indian."[24] This was a newsworthy, but not a particularly remarkable frontier event. No one knew or understood at the time that this constituted the setting of the fuse that would ignite the Nez Perce War three years hence. Ott's version was that the Indian, Eagle Robe, claimed ownership of Ott's land for sometime. On the day of the shooting, he tore down Ott's fence and then jumped in front of Ott's team while it was plowing and scared the horses by waving a blanket. He also threw a stone at Ott, striking him in the head. Thus provoked, Ott drew his six-shooter and fired. The slug

Figure. 3.22 This tree was planted in the 1860s. Photo by the author.

took effect in the side of one breast and ripped through both. Eagle Robe lingered six days before his death. Ott gave himself up to authorities and was apparently bound over for trial after an examination. "It is said the Indians were a little excited over the affair at first and were [unreadable] to blame Larry for the deed,

Figure. 3.23 Gravestone of Jeanette Manuel's mother, Margaret Popham at Slate Creek Cemetery. She died on 14 November 1869. Isabella was undoubtedly aware of the death of her friend's mother. Photo by the author.

as though it was his fault, but now seem satisfied that he had done right in shooting the way he did." The ethnocentrism displayed by the newspaper account here is simply overwhelming.

The white settlers in the area were wrought up over the recent redistricting that made Camas Prairie part of the new Idaho County, instead of Nez Perce County. The county seat was moved from Washington (AKA Warren's Diggings) to Mount Idaho. They were in no mood to worry about an Indian being shot, according to local historian Adkison.[25] A committee, which included Samuel Benedict, was set up to examine the shooting matter. Lacking legal authority, the committee did nothing. Indian anger and resentment continued to smolder.

The County commissioners gave Sam Benedict a franchise for building a ferry across Salmon River on April 1874.[26] They also set the rates he was allowed to charge: Horse or mule and rider, 75 cents, horse packed, 50 cents, loose and light horses, 25 cents, cattle per head, 25 cents, hogs and sheep 12-and-a-half cents each, and foot men, 25 cents.

In 1875, President Grant rescinded his 1873 order giving half the Wallowa Valley to the Nez Perce Band that had lived there from time immemorial. They were told they must leave and allow the entire site

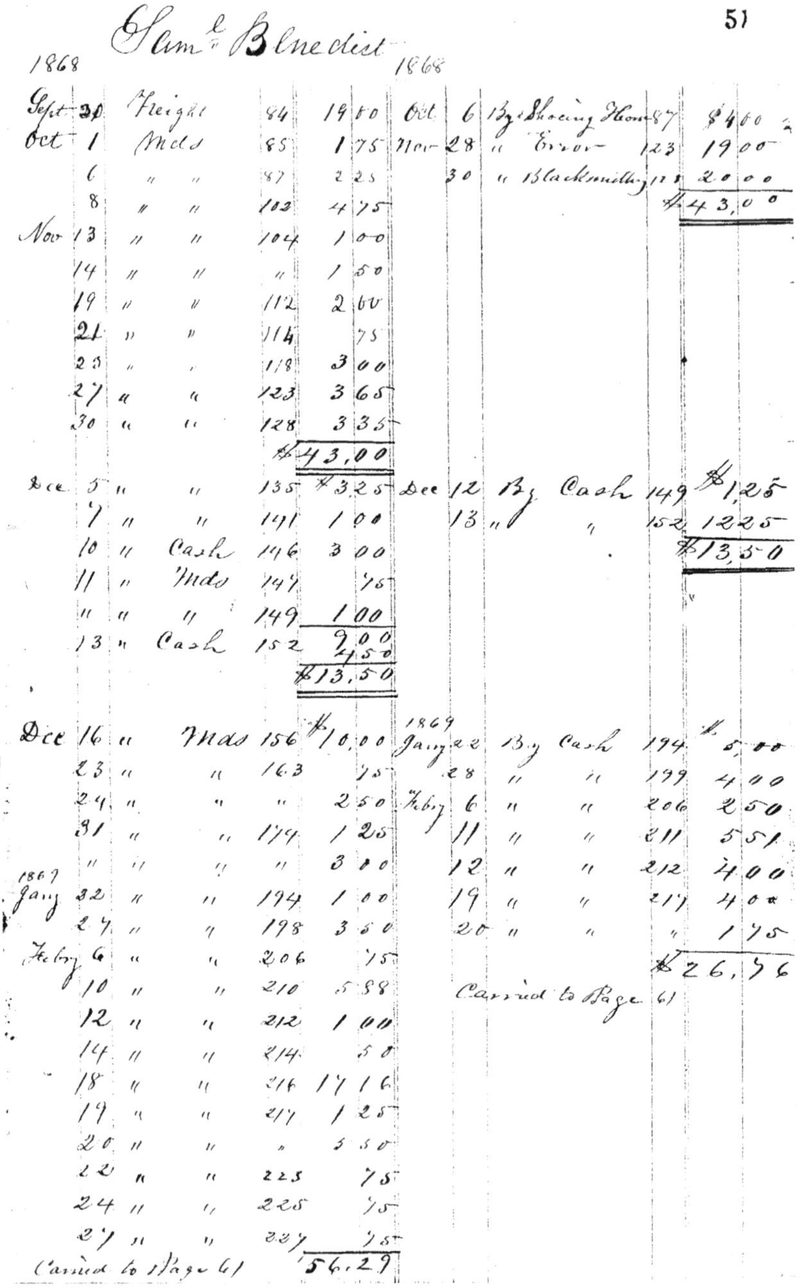

Sam.ˡ Benedict

1868   1868   51

Figure. 3.24 Ledger page from the Benedict store business records. Records are held at the Historical Museum at St. Gertrude's, Cottonwood, Idaho. Photo from the collection of Deborah Starr.

Figure 3.25 White Bird Village during a flood. Photo from collection of Deb Starr.

of breath-taking beauty to the settlers. Would the Nez Perce leave peaceably, fight, or what? This was a question of importance to the whole Northwest.

In late August of 1875, an incident occurred at the Benedict store in which a Native American died. As with so many other events, the various retellings differed remarkably. In April of 1878, after the war, Isabella wrote a long letter to the Lewiston Teller explaining her recollections.[27] The following paragraphs paraphrase, but closely follow, her letter.

Five Indians came down the Salmon that Sunday, each had a bottle of whiskey which they said they got at John Days. (This was a store there which was a few miles up the Salmon from the Benedict store.) Young Mox Mox wanted little Charles Cone to give him bullets to load his pistol. Cone said he had none, so the men passed the Benedict store and went on to Charley Schneider's store. They soon returned. John Manuel met them and talked to them. At Benedict's, they dismounted and sat down on a small hill in back of the Benedict home.

Mr. Benedict was working in his shop at the time. The little Benedict daughter, Frances, went to the door to see them and Mox Mox pointed his pistol at her. She ran to tell her mother, who went to the

*Figure. 3.26 Glatigny ranch near White Bird Creek and Salmon River. This shows
the geography of that area. Photo from the collection of Deborah Starr.*

door to see the Nez Perce men. They had their knives drawn. They
asked Mrs. Benedict to go into the melon patch and get them some
melons. She believed they were drunk and told them to ask her husband for the melons. She went back inside the house. They must have
gone into the patch and helped themselves, as some of the pickets of
the fence were broken off and melons in the patch were cut. Later,
Mr. Benedict told his wife that he thought she had given them melons
since he saw them seated and eating them. Mrs. Benedict was reading
in the house and did not notice when they went away.

About nine o'clock that night, they returned when the Benedict's
were in bed but still awake reading. They heard a noise and Sam went
to inspect. He reported that a window at the store was raised halfway
up. He went to get boards, hammer and nails and nailed down the
windows. He then took his gun and went to the corn field where he
saw the Indians going up the road. He went back to his wife and told
her not to be frightened as he did not think they would come back.
He fell asleep, but Isabella could not sleep.

About midnight, the Nez Perce men returned shooting, throwing
rocks and screaming like wild demons. Sam woke up and said not to

light the lamp. He got up and took his gun which was loaded with fine bird shot and went out and shot at the men. Afterwards, Mrs. Benedict said, they learned that some of the bird shot hit Stick in the Mud in the side, and one or two pellets hit young Mox Mox in the head. Sam then went back inside and did no more shooting that night. He had no powder or shot in the house with which to reload. He wanted Isabella and the children to go and hide in the brush while he would get an ax and be prepared to defend his house with that. Isabella was afraid he would get killed in such a fight, and successfully begged him to go hide with the rest of his family.

The whole family quietly got out the back, went up White Bird Creek and waded across to the side opposite the store. The Indians noticed them missing and began to look for them. Then Benedict saw the Indians and believed the Indians had spotted them too. The family hid behind some brush in the back of the ditch and made their way as best they could up to the China claim where they halted. It was 3 o'clock in the morning and Mrs. Benedict was wet through from wading the creek and falling down several times. She laid down in her wet night clothes. Mr. Benedict took two "Chinamen" with him

Figure. 3.27 The village of White Bird after a great fire.
Photo from the collection of Deborah Starr.

and they all crossed the river again to the cabin of some Frenchmen living there. They told these men what had happened. The Frenchmen went to the Benedict store and stayed there the rest of the night.

In the morning, the men wanted to hang the Indians, but Mr. Benedict would have nothing to do with hanging them. He said whoever gave them the whiskey was as bad as the Indians. They sent word

Figure. 3.28 1910 Independence Day in White Bird Village.
Photo from the collection of Deborah Starr.

to the Indian agent at Lapwai but he paid no attention. The Benedicts' door and windows were broken and their porch and yard were strewn with rocks the native men had thrown at the house. There was an Indian killed, but who killed him, she did not know. He had been shot with a pistol ball and neither of the Benedicts had a pistol or pistol ball. She believed that he must have been killed by another Indian through mistake or else he shot himself in the drunken row. Mr. Dupost first found the body and said the pistol was so close the shot burned his shirt. They asked the Indians who owned the pistol and they said it belonged to the dead man. Later, they wanted it back, but Benedict would not give it to them as he believed it might be needed for evidence if a trial resulted.

Isabella said she did not recover from the fright of that night for over a year and felt she could no longer live there. Her sister and brother-in-law tried to get Sam to leave but he felt he could not. The Benedict family had a good house and were beginning to make some money. She had just gotten over her fright when the 1877 troubles began. Her husband signed the petition for the removal of the Indians to the reservation to go along with the other settlers, although he was personally indifferent to the idea. General Howard had read the petition signers' names to the Indians in council at Lapwai. The signers included James Baker and John Manuel. The General thus had pointed out to the Indians their victims for revenge. The Nez Perce to be removed were not those in the Wallowa Valley, but the bands that frequented the Whitebird Creek and Salmon River area.

In Bailey's *River of No Return*, 1935 (p. 205) Grant Benedict said that the Indians broke into the Benedict store and stole a copper kettle full of whiskey. Benedict used up all his ammunition in the row, which ensued, and killed the Umatilla and wounded all the others. At one point, more than 100 Frenchmen kept a guard at the Benedict store for several days and nights. The incident had grown in the oral history through the years.

The Indians viewed this as another incident, much like the killing by Ott, that showed the Nez Perce would not get justice. Two settlers

Figure. 3.29 White Bird village set in the deep canyon of Whitebird Creek. Photo from the collection of Deborah Starr.

in the Wallowa area killed a Nez Perce man, Wilhautyah, at Whiskey Creek about this same time. They were not convicted either. Settlers killed somewhere between 28 and 32 Nez Perce, according to historian McDermott.[28]

In 1876, as America's one-hundredth fourth of July approached, and the Nation was celebrating in Philadelphia with a grand exposition, word arrived that Custer and his entire command had been wiped out on the Great Plains. The word of the battle went west also and reached the Nez Perce and their allied tribes quickly. The cavalry was not invincible; armed resistance was possible; and surrender was not the only option. These were near to revelations. The Nez Perce living in the Wallowa Valley of Oregon were told to move to Lapwai. Meetings and negotiations went on in Wallowa during late 1876 with General Oliver Otis Howard the senior commanding officer. At last, the leaders of that band, particularly Chief Joseph, felt they had no option and they began to cross the run-off swollen Snake River with their young and old people, horse herds and all they owned. This event induced great resentment, anger, and perhaps thoughts of trying the path Crazy Horse had chosen for his people.

Daughter, Frances Benedict, remembered that an Indian boy "with whom we played told us the Indians would fight if they were forced to go to the reservation."[29] Mr. Chamberlain remembered that people who had not signed the petition to remove the Indians were warned of the impending trouble.[30] In April of that year, Harry Mason, who lived in the same area as the Benedicts, whipped two Nez Perce. He was not punished either.

The final council between Howard and Joseph in May ended with the Indians given 30 days to relocate. By 1877, there were more than enough problems, resentments, and fears to kindle a possible blaze of conflict between the settlers and the natives. As the long warm days of summer approached the deep canyon of the River of No Return, the Benedict family, was at the epicenter of impending conflict.

End Notes

[1] DeVeny, Betty. "Slate Creek History," Typescript, March 1974. DeVeny said that George Popham, Jeanette's father was on the jury. This would be the earliest reference to that family being in Florence. Orlando "Rube" Robbins was also said to be on the first jury ever called in Idaho.

[2] Brocky is sometimes seen spelled "Brockie."

[3] Ted Van Arsdol, "*The Lewiston Journal, 1867-1872*," *Echoes of the Past*, Oct. 2010, p. 19.

[4] Boise County Marriage Records.

[5] Family Search Genealogical site, internet. Located 1/11/2009.

[6] Mills, Nellie Ireton. *All Along the River: Territorial and Pioneer Days on the Payette*. Montreal: Payette Radio Limited, 1963. P. 219. Mills erroneously says Isabella's first husband was Jack Manuel.

[7] "Three Pioneer Women of Idaho, Who Have Had Various and Thrilling Experiences," *Idaho Daily Statesman*, 23 July 1911, Section II, p. 3.

[8] *Idaho World*, Idaho City, 9 October 1888, p. 1, c. 3-4.

[9] *Idaho World*, Idaho City, 17 October 1868, p. 3.

[10] *Idaho Statesman*, Boise, Idaho, 20 October, 1868, p. 2, c. 1.

[11] *Semi-Weekly Idaho World*, Idaho City, 21 October, 1868, p. 2, c. 3.

[12] *Semi-Weekly Idaho World*, Idaho City, 21 October, 1868, p. 2, c. 3.

[13] *Idaho World*, Idaho City, 21 November, 1868, p. 3, c. 3.

[14] Idaho County Marriage Records. This marriage does not loom large in the family collective memory. At first I thought this was Isabella's sister who had quickly rid herself of Mr. Dougherty, but it was not.

[15] *Oregonian*, Portland, Oregon, 18 January 1870, p. 2.

[16] Eighteen months after this lynching, a man named Walters was lynched in Lewiston, according to the *Oregonian* newspaper of 21 June 1921.

[17] *Idaho Statesman*, 1 February 1870, p. 2, c. 2, 3. Spellings have been modernized here.

[18] Copy in author's possession.

[19] Copy of the letter in author's possession.

[20] Docket Book, Florence, Idaho, p. 138. Olson Manuscript Collection, University of Idaho, Special Collections.

[21] Claim No. 10557, Court of Claims, Abstract of evidence dated 10 May 1898.

[22] *Idaho Signal*, Lewiston, 8 March 1873, p. 3, c. 3.

[23] *Idaho Signal*, Lewiston, 8 March 1873, p. 3, c. 3.

[24] *Idaho Signal*, Lewiston, 28 March 1874, p. 3, c. 1.

[25] J. Loyal Adkison, "Benedict Family Closely Related to Early Idaho County History." *Idaho County Free Press*, Grangeville, Idaho, 27 March 1952.

[26] Notes, no citation, but says Record of County Commissioners, 9 April 1874.

[27] *Lewiston Teller*, 26 April 1878, p. 1, c. 5-6. Letter from Mrs. S. Benedict from Grangeville, dated 17 April.

[28] McDermott, *Forlorn Hope*, fn. 7, p. 39.

[29] Frances I. (Benedict) Shissler. *Bonners Ferry Herald*, Bonners Ferry, Idaho. 6 April 1939, p. 1, c.1 & 2, p. 6, c. 2 & 3.

[30] *History of North Idaho*, 1903, Biography of Chamberlain.

4

START OF THE NEZ PERCE WAR

May-June 1877

In May of 1877, Sitting Bull's band of Lakota (Sioux) went north to Canada to avoid the relentless pursuit of the cavalry seeking to capture and punish the winners of the Battle of Little Big Horn. Sanctuary in the country they called the "Grandmother Land" was a new concept for Indians, but one destined to spread. On May 31, the Wallowa Band of Nez Perce crossed the still swollen Snake River at Dug Bar and were well on their way to their new reservation. By June 3, five bands of Non-treaty Nez Perce gathered at Tolo Lake on the Camas Prairie. Joseph, White Bird, Looking Glass, Toolhoolhoolzote, and Husishusis Kute headed those bands. The women gathered camas bulbs and the men made council. Tolo Lake was, and remains, just a few miles from Mount Idaho and the fledgling settlement of Grangeville but several miles and many feet of altitude from the Benedict store below on the River of No Return.[1]

A few days before the Nez Perce War started in June of 1877, Samuel Benedict stopped at Tolo Lake on his way home from Mount Idaho to inquire about purchasing some ponies from the Indians who were camped there.[2] Nez Perce were famously successful at breeding outstanding horses. They were holding a council of war, saying they were angry and intended to fight, according to Benedict's daughter Frances' later memory. They ordered Benedict to leave. Camping at this spot was a regular summer tradition, but the eviction from the

Wallowa Valley made the summer of 1877 not at all ordinary. Later that day, as Benedict approached his home near the mouth of White Bird Creek at the Salmon River, he was joined by Mox Mox, one of the Nez Perce camped nearby. Another traditional local camping spot for that season was up White Bird Creek near the Manuel ranch. Mox Mox returned with Benedict to his home where they gave him food, which was not unusual in any way. He strolled around the yard for several hours which aroused no suspicion from the Benedicts at the time. Later, the Benedicts believed he had been planning the attack on their home.

Another inkling of impending trouble came to the Benedicts from an aged Indian man they had dubbed "Old Fisherman."[3] He was of undetermined ancient age and regularly stopped at the Benedict place every few days as part of his fishing jaunts to the Salmon River. Isabella fed him, and at times he stayed there over night.

He was a member of another Northwest tribe, not the Nez Perce, and spoke only a few words of English. He came by that day in the early afternoon and Isabella fed him. He sat on the floor but showed no appetite. He tried to tell Isabella to go away. "Take papoose and cla-ta-wa," he said and made motions by holding his arms like a gun and saying boom, boom as he pointed at each of the family members.[4] He stayed the night but they never saw him again after that visit. The older two Benedict children, Grant and Caddie, were at school in Mount Idaho, staying with the Rudolph family, and the two youger ones, Addie and Frances, were at home.

Figure 4.1 *Headstone of William Osborn. Photo by author, Oct. 2011. This is in the French Cemetery. Osborn was one of the first to die when the war started.*

The first raiding party of the Nez Perce War—Wahlitits or

*Figure 4.2 Osborn cemetery plot with the
Photo by author, Oct. 2011.*

Wahlietiits (Shore Cross-
ing), his cousin Sarpsis
Ilppilp (Red Moccasin
Tops), and his 17-year-
old nephew Wetyet-
mas Wahyakt (Swan
Necklace)—stopped at
the Manuel ranch on
Wednesday, June 13, to
sharpen their knives on the foot-powered stone there.[5] They were
traveling down the White Bird hill trail from the Camas Prairie to
the Salmon River. They did not molest the Manuel family at that
time, and Jack Manuel later reported that he felt no sense of threat
or impending danger.[6] The Manuel family had good relations with
the Indians and the Nez Perce were frequent visitors.

Thursday 14 June 1877

Their chief target was Larry Ott, slayer of Eagle Robe, but he could not
be found. After attacking and killing Richard Devine, "Harry" Burn
Breckrodge, Robert Bland, and Jurgen Henry Elfers upstream along
the Salmon River, the trio of Nez Perce went on to Samuel Benedict's
store, arriving the next morning, Thursday, June 14.[7] Sam Benedict
was busy tending to his livestock that morning because his hired hand,
Edgar Hall, had left the day before to work on a project near by.[8] As
Sam started to ride out to his field, he saw three Nez Perce approaching. He returned to his house and sat on the porch pretending to read
as he closely observed the men. They rode up to him and asked if they
could use the lower road which went around Benedict's garden fence
and under a bluff in times of low water in the river. He told them it
was impassable, and they went on up the Salmon River. Benedict then
mounted his horse to go at last to check on the cows with new calves,
or according to another version to round up his horses.[9]

Red Moccasin Tops was especially anxious to even the score from
having been wounded by Benedict the year before. When they shot

Benedict in his pasture, he played dead, and they returned to their camp on Camas Prairie to share the news of their attack of vengeance.

Later in the day Benedict returned home, but he was riding bareback on a bridle-less work horse owned by neighbor James Baker. Benedict also had removed his riding boots. Isabella and her daughter thought maybe he had been bit by a rattlesnake. "When I saw him coming, running his horses down a steep hill at fearful speed, I thought of Indians in an instant. Indeed, they never were absent from my mind—I always had feared them. But, of late, I knew by their actions that they meant mischief to somebody. Yet, they assured the settlers that they meant to make war only on the soldiers. As he neared the house, I saw that he sat his horse with difficulty, and ran to meet him. He was covered with blood."[10] "Oh, Sam, What's the matter?" Isabella asked.

Sam replied, "Don't get excited Belle. Those three Indians followed and shot me and the horse, leaving me for dead. After they left, I managed to mount the old horse which was near a rock and he brought me home." He had been shot in the hip, and horse and rider were a gore of blood. "I helped him to dismount, when he laid under a tree in the yard a moment. Then looking hurriedly around, he told his story, requesting me to help him into the house and send for Brown, who came, as already stated." Isabella assisted him into the house and on to a cot in the dining room. The older daughter, Frances, was sent to Brown's store about a mile down the Salmon to summon help. There she located John Doumecq who went back to her home with her. Doumecq left the Benedicts and returned home to get more men, and intended to return and spend the night but was too late to be able to return.

Figure 4.3 French Cemetery sign. This is near The White Bird Creek and Salmon River confluence. Photo by author.

Sam had Isabella pack two trunks with their best possessions to bury for safekeeping in case of more conflict. They had just put in a supply of merchandise worth about $1,500. Their account books had about $1,000 in outstanding bills owed to them. Storekeeper Brown came down before long and told Sam, "The Indians must have a grudge against you."[11] Benedict retorted, "You may think they have a grudge against you before the day is over. You see Brown, what these redskins have done. They will come back tonight and kill us all." Brown replied, "No, Benedict, I don't believe it. If they wanted to kill you they would have done it all at once."[12] Brown prescribed a cold water treatment for Benedict's wound and then went home. About 4 o'clock that afternoon Brown was reading on his porch when a cry from across the river said the Indians were coming.

> "After Brown's return home, I [Isabella] grew more anxious as
> time sped, especially as my husband's faith in the friendship
> of savages was broken by the ball that left him at their mercy,
> powerless to protect his own or our lives. He told Brown they
> meant to kill him, insisting that it was no personal grudge,
> that they meant war, and surely would come and kill us all. I
> sent my little girl for some Frenchmen, who were mining near
> by on the Salmon River. They returned with the child, but,
> like others, could not entertain a doubt of the Indians, and
> left their guns behind at their camp. Upon hearing my
> husband's statement, they started to return, promising to
> secure their guns, return, and stop all night with us. I could
> not bear to be left alone, and one of the men (August)
> stopped with us. I gave him a fine breech loader that belonged
> to Mr. Ruby (Robie) who had left it with my husband until he
> should return from a trip to Mount Idaho."[13]

Brown grabbed his hunting bag and Winchester rifle and handed a shotgun to his newly-arrived brother-in-law, Albert Benson. Benson had never fired a weapon in his life. They successfully crossed the river despite being slightly wounded and after a few adventures were rescued two weeks later. [14]

About six that evening, Benedict's Chinese cook was washing lettuce for supper, according to Frances's memory, when he heard the Indians coming and yelled: "Hi-yu! Indians!" Tim Taylor, great grandson of Sam and Isabella, said years later that this was wrong; he remembered that they had no such helper at the time. They had a Chinese cook later at John Day.[15] Isabella remembered that she had gone to the garden for lettuce and onions for dinner. Either she or Frances, the older daughter, ran to the house and told everyone, "There are lots of Indians coming!" Isabella took baby Addie from her bed. According to daughter, Frances (Mrs. Shissler), "The Indians dismounted at the gate and as they came toward the house were told to stay out by [Benedict's employee] August Bacon who had grabbed a gun, shut the door, and was standing firm by the door.[16] The painted Indians answered with a volley of shots and Mr. Bacon fell to the sitting room floor. He lay on his back, apparently dead. The Indians then entered the room and one of them cut Mr. Bacon's throat where he lay. Another, took off his cartridge belt, which was blood-soaked, and brought it into the kitchen where he made me clean it off in the wash basin."[17] Meanwhile Samuel Benedict somehow got up and told Isabella to take the children and get out of the house. She described it: "I said, 'What can I do?' My husband was on a bed in a small room that opened off the front room and had only a half-sash window opening into the back yard, near the creek, where the low

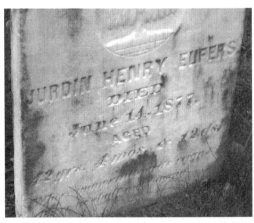

Figure 4.4 Headstone of Jurdin Henry Elfers, one of the first to die from the raid that lead to the Nez Perce War. Photo by author. Oct. 2011.

bank was lined with thick bushes and reeds. He told me to take the children and fly. I said, 'No, I won't leave you.' He replied, 'Think of the children, and save them!' I started, but, on reaching the back gate, saw some Indians watching me from the hillside, and returned to the house. (I had seen my husband leaning out of the window while I was in the yard with the children.) On entering my husband's room, I found it empty. Then, glancing into the front room, I saw August still barring the Indians' entrance. He had killed several, and, at the instant I looked, he fell backward into the house."[18] Benedict struggled to go outside and ran as best he could toward the creek. His daughter last saw him near the middle of the creek with the Nez Perce shooting at him. This event was also witnessed by European men who were at a safe distance across the river.[19] They were later able to add important details.

"I flew to the creek, and rushed with my children into the water. Crouching low among the reeds, we escaped their observation. Their triumph over the brave Frenchman had diverted them from my movements, and enabled me to escape. When all was still, I cautiously crept to the house under cover of the night.[20] August lay just as I had seen him fall. They had taken his gun and left his body unmolested. Satisfying themselves with the supper I had prepared they had hurried to other scenes of bloodshed and pillage. I could find no clue to my husband's whereabouts. I searched everywhere, and called his name, but could find no trace—only some blood stains on the window, as though he might have escaped through it. He never was found."[21]

Isabella took some money and trinkets, including a gold cross, and, with Frances and Addie, fled up White Bird Creek heading toward her old friend Jeanette at the Manuel ranch.[22] In a letter written 12 days after this, Isabella said, "They had their pistols and guns pointed at me several times, but there was one Indian who saved me and told me to go to Manuel's."[23] Later, Isabella recalled, "Covering August's body with a quilt, I left all that once was home, and set out with my little ones for Mount Idaho, where my older children were

Figure 4.5 *John Day Cemetery. Oct. 2011. Photo by the author.*

Figure 4.6 *View from John Day Cemetery. Photo by the author.*

in school . . ." As this distraught family went past the Baker place, they saw Baker's body with many arrows sticking out of his back. Unbeknownst to them, Baker and the Manuel family had been together when attacked, and Baker had been killed in the attack, while trying to help the Manuels.

Apparently, Benedict waited until his wife and children were hidden in the creek-bank brush, and then crawled out the window of his home. He limped along as best he could, using the strength he developed in his years of blacksmithing. In the middle of the footbridge spanning White Bird Creek, he was hit with a volley of fire and fell dead into the rushing water.[24]

Later that evening, Mrs. Katherine Osborn saw her husband and other relatives murdered before she took the children and ran to safety at the home of John Wood at Slate Creek. Wood was the brother of Isabella's late step-father.[25] Elsewhere in the area that day, Helen J. Walsh, widowed sister of Harry Mason, heard three men talking in her brother's store about five miles upriver from Whitebird.[26] One of the men, Bill George was sent to warn the Benedicts, Manuels and Mr. Baker on Whitebird Creek that the Indians had risen. Mason asked them to come to his store, as he believed it was very safe. Soon Mr. George returned with an invitation from Mr. Baker for everyone to come to his house, which had a strong stone cellar for defense. Most horses were out grazing and only three could be rapidly obtained to transport 12 people. Mrs. Osborne was especially slow in getting going and the whole party could not leave until nearly 7 o'clock. Harry Mason, local storekeeper, led this group of 10 toward James Baker's cabin seeking protection. They passed by the Benedict home on the opposite side of Whitebird Creek before being turned back. This must have been shortly after Isabella and her children left. The Mason party immediately ran into a group of Nez Perce men. Later, the men were killed and the women and children ended up at the makeshift fort at Slate Creek.

According to some accounts, the little Benedict group saw J. J. Manuel laying by the fence of his yard and thought him dead. This is unlikely, since he had previous gone deep into the brush for safety and was not mobile enough to move further. Just before they reached the Manuel home, Isabella and her two children encountered George Popham, Jeanette's father, who was coming in from the Manuel pasture. Popham had been living with the Manuels for months. He told them excitedly that Jack Manuel had been shot. Isabella implored him to try to reach Mount Idaho and bring help. Popham replied, "My good woman, we would all be murdered, and there is no use to go."[27]

The Benedict family found Mrs. Manuel and her two children on the back porch of the Manuel home, and Jeanette raised her skirt and said, "Look, Belle, what they did to me!" She exposed a deep cut on her knee. Popham suggested Jeanette go to her husband to bid him goodbye, and she put her baby in Isabella's arms and left with her father. They doubted Jack Manuel would survive the night. Jeanette came back about dark, just as Indians were seen approaching. Isabella wrote, "while I was standing there talking five or six Indians came along and we just had time to hide in the brush when they got to the house."[28] From Frances's account: "More Indians were seen approaching and we immediately hid in the brush near the creek on a low flat, where we all spent the night, expecting to be killed any minute!"[29] Again, from Maggie's account: "That night mother, the baby, myself, Mrs. Benedict and the men stayed in the brush." While both families hid that night in the brush, at one point they heard someone chopping wood and someone saying "Hello." They surmised it was a Nez Perce man trying to decoy them out of the brush and back to the ranch. They did not respond. Frances remembered that her mother "remained hidden all day, gradually working her way through the brush to the end of the meadow."

Isabella learned from the survivors what had befallen the Manuel family earlier that first day of conflict. Just before noon that day, Thursday, the 14th, their mutual neighbor, James Baker, came to the Manuel ranch with the news that Sam Benedict had been wounded. Baker had apparently learned this from Bill George.[30] Jack Manuel sent Baker back home. Soon Baker returned though, and they all decided to go to Mr. Baker's stone cellar, about a mile down the creek. It was easily defended. George Popham went to the pasture to find a horse to ride, and the others left immediately without waiting for him.

Six-year-old, Maggie Manuel, mounted her father's horse behind him, while Jeanette and the baby, John Jr., took another animal. They had proceeded about half a mile when looking to a hill they saw several Indians coming toward them on the run, yelling and whooping at the top of their voices. "The Indians are coming," Maggie said to her father. Just as the Indians appeared, the Manuel horses became frightened at the noise and stampeded, separating Jack from Jeanette. Baker, meanwhile, was shot and fell from his horse. The Indians opened fire on Jack and Maggie with arrows, the first arrow striking Maggie's left arm near the shoulder. Next, an arrow struck Maggie in the back of the head and glanced and pierced her father's neck. An Indian fired a gun at Jack, at the same time, and shot him through the hips. A second bullet burned one of his ears. The wound through the hips caused him to fall from the horse, dragging Maggie with him. Jack saw that their only chance was to roll down the hillside into the brush, and this they did, meanwhile undergoing rock throwing from the Indians. One rock broke Jack's little finger, and another struck Maggie on the forehead. The Indians were afraid to follow them, doubtless thinking that Jack still had his pistols. Manuel had left all weapons and ammunition at the house, with the idea of showing the Indians they might meet that they were peaceable.

Jeanette's frightened horse threw her with the baby, and in the fall one of her kneecaps was cut and broken, and the baby injured. Popham said his daughter was raped at this point, but he was a self-contradictory witness. Such an attack was most unlikely. Two or three of the Indians took her back to her house and promised not to harm her if she would give up the ammunition and a fine rifle that Jack had. She did this and was uninjured by her captors. As soon as the Indians left the place, George Popham, who had remained concealed, came into the house. Jeanette told him where Jack and Maggie had crawled and he went to find them. He brought Maggie to the house, and left blankets, water, and possibly some food for Jack Manuel. Isabella said later the Indians had taken all of the food, so there may not have been any taken to Jack Manuel. Then the Benedicts arrived.

Grant Benedict and the People at Mount Idaho

At Mount Idaho, where Grant Benedict and his sister, Caddie, were living with the Rudolph family while attending school, settlers from the area began to pour into town seeking safety.[31] School was dismissed; all hands, young and old, began to fortify their location. The arriving settlers brought word of the death of Grant's father. Through his grief, Grant wanted to go to his mother and sisters to see if he could help. The people of Mount Idaho wisely would not allow him to undertake this impossible mission.

Friday 15 June 1877

The next morning Isabella tried to persuade Jeanette to go up the creek and escape to the prairie, but Jeanette and her father George Popham decided to return to the house, thinking the danger was over. Jeanette also refused to leave her husband alone in the brush, wounded and without aid.[32] In addition, her own knee injury made her an unlikely candidate for a difficult hike.

Isabella later recalled, "The Indians had eaten every morsel in the house before they left and I could not even get a crust at Mrs. Manuel's."[33] This contradicts the statements that food had been taken to Jack Manuel at his hiding place.

Figure 4.7 Chapman Creek sign near where the Manuel ranch was located. Photo by the author. According to Mike Peterson, Seth Jones owned the old Manuel property in the early Twentieth Century. Later, it was owned by Cone, then Bent Brothers, and in 1979 bought by Anderson, Robinson and Zumwalt.

Isabella and Jeanette said goodbye for the last time. On Friday night, as Frances remembered, the family continued on their way toward Mount Idaho and stayed close to the road.[34] At Mount Idaho, Grant got up from a sleepless night to face still more stress and reason to fear for his family.[35] Friday morning, the Norton family wagon came into Mount Idaho. Joe Moore and Lew Day were mortally wounded. Later, the Chamberlain wagon came in with the husband and small son dead.

Grant was close enough to hear the message L.P. Brown sent to the commanding officer at Fort Lapwai. It read: "The Indians have possession of the prairie, and threaten Mount Idaho. All the people are here. Give us relief, arms and ammunition. I fear all the people on Salmon River are killed. Hurry up; hurry! Rely on this Indian. I have known him a long time." The Nez Perce man in question was a brother of Chief Looking Glass who later sided with Chief Joseph and the Non-treaty Nez Perce.

Grant worked feverishly all day with the men to reinforce their makeshift fort. He carried sacks of flour from Brown's mill up the hill. That night, one of the guards exchanged gunfire with some Nez Perce and all the settlers scrambled to the makeshift fort. To bring calm to the group two men led them singing old-time songs.

Back at the Benedict store, everything was smashed or taken, and the whiskey supply—probably hundreds of gallons—was taken. Many of the wilder moments over the next few days were blamed on this whiskey. At some point, the Benedict house and store were burned.

Back at the Manuel Ranch

Isabella had plenty of immediate worries but must have also had fears for her life-long friend Jeanette that she left at the Manuel ranch. They would never meet again. Jeanette was never seen after Saturday evening. Little Maggie Manuel told a tale of seeing her mother stabbed to death by a Nez Perce man whom she believed was Chief Joseph. The other detailed version of her death surfaced later that year. Contemporary writer, Duncan McDonald, made the most detailed accusations about the killing of Jeanette and they were based on interviews a few months later with Indian men who claimed to have been there. McDonald claimed that on Sunday morning Mrs. Manuel was hiding in the upstairs loft when the Indians burned the house shortly after the battle of Whitebird.[36] After the war, the *New Northwest*, of Deer Lodge, Montana, commissioned him to go to Canada and spend time with the Nez Perce who had escaped there, and then tell the story of the war from the Indian viewpoint. It is unclear just who he talked to and how close to the events those informants really were. The following is his version.

> "The other white woman was burned in a house with her child. When her husband and others were murdered by the Nez Perces, she went upstairs. The Indians say they did not see her at the time of killing the men. When the Indians got possession of the house Joseph, Jr. [Chief Joseph] was present. He was sitting at one side of the place smoking his pipe. He was asked by the warriors what should be done—whether they should set fire to the house or leave without destroying it. All this time the woman and child were upstairs, but they Indians say they did not know it. Young (Chief) Joseph answered, "You have done worse deeds than burning a house. You never asked our chiefs what was best to be done. You have murdered many men and not asked advice of your chiefs. You can do as you please about the house.

Some of the young men lit a match and set fire to the building. They then went back a little and sat down to watch it burn. They were suddenly startled by the piercing screams of a woman in the second story of the house. Chief Joseph ordered them to put out the fire. The young Indians ran down to the water, filled their hats, threw it on the flames, and tried every way they knew to extinguish the fire and save the woman. But it was too late. She and her child perished.

The same young warriors who were with Joseph at the time told me that when he left the place, Joseph held down his head for a long time and, at last looking up, he said they had done very wrong in burning the woman, that he was very sorry, that he had believed the house empty.[37]

One important detail was that the Manuel home was only one story high. The part about carrying water in hats seems strange since the Manuels had a well in the yard and the creek was some distance away. Why would the Nez Perce men carry water in their hats instead of go inside and try to rescue Jeanette if rescuing her was their goal? Whoever related this story to McDonald seemed to be trying to partially exonerate the Nez Perce rather than tell a factual story. Apparently, McDonald's main source was his relative, Chief White Bird himself. Almost everyone agrees that Joseph did not arrive in that area until much later that day. Also, Frederick Brice (aka Pat Price) entered the home on Sunday morning, just after the battle, and did not see or hear Jeanette or her infant.

Jack Manuel was listed with the dead in the Lewiston newspaper on June 23.[38] On June 29th the report came out that Jack Manuel was not dead. Reports in Portland and other points contained a report on June 30.[39] This did not name Jack Manuel, but said "we found and brought into camp one of the settlers, reported dead after the massacre on the Salmon River. He is wounded in two places and almost starved. He has now a fair prospect for recovery." The Lewiston newspaper said "J. J. Manuel was found wounded in the hips and between the shoulders, secreted 13 days after being wounded and subsisted on turnips and berries, thinks he will recover."[40]

Manuel told a harrowing tale.[41] The first night after the attack he had played dead, and two Nez Perce spread their blankets within 20 feet of where he lay. Jack heard their breathing but was so badly wounded he was unable to move. In the morning, they took a drink of whiskey from a bottle they had, and moved away. Jack made a superhuman effort and crawled further into the brush. The braves returned and discovered his warm blanket, but did not find him. After five days, when everyone had

Figure 4.8 Headstone of James Baker who was killed while trying to escape with the Manuel family. Isabella worked for him for several years, and saw his body on the road as she approached the Manuel house on the first part of her escape. Mt. Idaho Cemetery. Photo by author.

left the area, Jack was able to reach the arrowhead in his neck and with the aid of a hunting knife, pull it out himself. He treated the wound with a homemade compress of horseradish leaves.

Maggie's version of the events of the night of June 16-17, 1877: "My first impulse [after seeing her mother and brother killed] was to find grandfather and I started in search of him. Instead of him, however, I found Pat Price (Frederick Brice), with whom I stayed in the brush that night. In the morning the Indians attacked Mr. Price and me in the brush. He determined to go straight to them and try a ruse … He then proposed to the Indians that if they would allow him to take me to Mount Idaho he would return and surrender himself to them. This the chief agreed to and … we left for the prairie."[42]

In Bailey's, River of No Return, there is a long narrative poem of this incident written by Miss Nannie Fabrique.[43] It described the Nez Perce as a "ruthless band," while Brice was described as "free from vice" and a member of the "Celtic race." That probably explained the writer's perspective as well as anything could.

In an interview in 1925, and another in 1944, Maggie told the now-legendary story that Brice opened his shirt to exhibit his tattoo of a Christian cross, and this so impressed the Indians that he was allowed to leave.[44] This became a very popular legend in the West and has been retold often. The story is notably absent from contemporary reports. Maggie seemed to add things she had heard to her own memories. In later years, she said Chief White Bird was with this group that stopped them.[45] She had met him before, perhaps many times, when his band camped on the Manuel ranch.

The Indian memory of this event is quite different. Black Feather (Whylimex) said he was on White Bird Creek in the forenoon when he saw a person crawling through the brush.[46] "Soon a person came into view and I recognized a white man. I saw on his left arm a child he was carrying . . . That white man nodded his head at me, a "how-do-you do." The first words I understood him say, was "Will you kill me?" I answered, "No." I had a gun, a rifle. I turned and walked to the three men smoking. Close behind me came the white man with the child on his arm ... When I approached near the smokers, the one facing me, Loppee Kasun [Two Mornings], an oldish man, sprang up pointing his gun ready to fire, trying to make a shot past me. One of the other men, all of them past middle age, spoke to Loppee, "Hold there! Do not shoot! Can you not see the child in his arms?"

When he reached the thicket, he turned and nodded to me, then disappeared in the brush. I saw him no more. I now said to Loppee, "If you shoot the man, who can care for the child? Would you carry it?"[47]

Whylimlex said that Brice, "showed no markings on his body anywhere."[48] As McWhorter points out, traditional Nez Perces do not recognize the cross nor worship it but they were accustomed to paintings and markings on the body.[49] There was no reason the display of a cross tattoo would be effective. This story of the cross was apparently so culturally satisfying that it was retold and elaborated upon until it became an irreproachable legend. Even Maggie, as we

Figure 4.9 Painting of Jeanette Manuel and her son trying to escape. By Liz Hess.

have seen, incorpo-
rated it into her later
memories. Elias Darr,
Grangeville black-
smith and Civil War
veteran, was among
the principal spread-
ers of the legend.[50]

Brice, carrying
Maggie in a box he
fashioned into a back-
pack, departed about
3 p.m., Sunday, the
17th, after the Battle
of White Bird. In Sep-
tember, less than three
months later, Brice
journeyed to Boise, en
route to Idaho City,

*Figure 4.10 Portrait of Maggie Manuel Bowman.
Some people have speculated that this is actually a
portrait of her mother Jeanette. That is unlikely.
Photo from the collection of Deborah Starr.*

and related his tale to the Boise newspaper.[51] He mentioned that he
had told the Indians they could kill him, but they let him go. He did
not mention the tattoo, or the shirt-ripping theatrics. The box he
carried her in was not constructed until the second day in most accounts. His memories were fresh at this time, and I judge them to be
the most reliable of his several accounts given over the years.

Brice had been without food for five days and was near exhaustion when his mission of mercy began, according to his frail memory.
However, there is no way to fit five days between the time he was first
surrounded by the Nez Perce war party and Sunday afternoon when
the trek to Mount Idaho began. He entered the Manuel house before
leaving for Mount Idaho, but found it empty—no bodies, no bloody
floor, no bloody little girl foot tracks—none of the elements that
crept into the narrative later.[52] He had to stop for rest frequently as he
carried the injured girl up the enormously steep White Bird Grade.

Maggie pointed out slain cavalry men to him as they traveled. The battle of White Bird, the first engagement to involve the army, had been fought there within a mile of the Manuel home, and the cavalry had been totally outperformed. One slain cavalryman was propped against a thorn bush so that the thorns kept him from falling. Another, had his brains exposed and part of his head severed. There was no evidence of deliberate mutilations, and the Nez Perce were later praised for their civilized conduct in battle. Supposedly there were 33 enlisted men of the First Cavalry slain there.[53] Apparently Brice followed the old wagon road up the mountain. Sunday night they reached the Harris ranch near the head of Rocky Canyon. Dark is not until after 9 p.m. that time of year. Brice found some food at the ransacked place and cooked supper. He also found a dry goods box he fashioned into a better conveyance for Maggie.[54] In the morning he strapped this on his back for the final day's journey. Maggie's broken, arrow-pierced arm was swollen, but despite these and other wounds she did not cry or murmur, Brice said. Shock, as much as bravery, may have been the cause of her stoicism. By the time of Brice's retelling, she was physically healed but Brice predicted with uncanny accuracy that "she will carry with her through life a vivid recollection of the terrible scenes and sufferings through which she has passed …"[55]

The term was undeveloped in the 1870s and the affliction undiagnosed and unrecognized, but the distinct possibility that little Maggie developed Post-Traumatic Stress Disorder must be considered. Modern estimates are that 60 to 80 percent of individuals who suffer trauma develop the disorder. More details of her subsequent childhood would be needed to make this kind of assessment with any certainty.

In her 1944 interview, Maggie said they stopped one night on this trip at Tolo Lake. This would not be on a direct route or close to one. The Nez Perce traditionally camped at Tolo for summer sports, but had moved their camp when the war began. Neither was this route mentioned in other accounts; it was yet another intrusive memory.

In Hailey's *History of Idaho* (1910) there was a reprint of the escape story as Brice told it to the Butte Inter-Mountain, and the Lewiston Tribune copied it.[56] It was apparently written about 1909 or so, 33 years after the event. Brice said he was on his way to Warren with a usual prospector's outfit and had not heard of any trouble with the Indians. He was overtaken and captured by a group of 25 Nez Perce. They wanted to kill him, but a Nez Perce man he knew interceded on his behalf and told Brice to hide in the brush. This he did and stayed there quietly until dark. It must have been the evening of Saturday, June 16. He only mentions one night hiding, and there is no reason he should have been starving for five days as he also reported. He followed the bed of White Bird Creek but had only gone a short distance when he heard a child sobbing, crying, and calling to her mother in English. This proved to be Maggie Manuel.

He said that from what the little girl told him, she thought her people were dead. "Her mother and an infant at breast had been killed outright at the cabin…" The father had been left for dead, lived on raw turnips, and then "he died, however, some two years later of exposure and the injuries received at the time." Brice was badly in error on this point. Maggie tried to run away at first but he talked to her and she went to sleep. When the sun arose, Brice discovered Maggie was hurt and he bound her wounds with his shirt and made her a dress of his undershirt. His coat and vest had been taken by the Indians the previous day. Maggie must have left the house fairly early in the evening after only a fitful, nightmare-filled nap.

During the morning (Sunday, 17 June 1877) there was a great commotion which Brice later learned was Colonel Perry's attack at White Bird. The Nez Perce were positioned between Brice and Maggie and the soldiers. Brice and Maggie stayed there three days and had no food but plenty of creek water, according to Brice's later account. Since he left for Mount Idaho Sunday afternoon, there is no way that they could have been there even one more day. His memory obviously became cloudy on this detail. By then, Brice was desperate and crawled through the brush until he saw three chieftains a few hundred yards away near a cabin. It's unclear if this was the Manuel home. He said White Bird was one of the Indians and "I have often wondered if one was not Chief Joseph himself." Brice told them he had a child with him. He said he was ready to die and they then told him to get the papoose and take her to her friends. There was a mention of the cross tattoo in parenthesis in the story as if the author added it. Brice himself had not adopted the tattoo cross story even by this late date.

Brice took off after these events and covered five miles by dark. The trail from White Bird to Mount Idaho is incredibly steep and this seemingly short journey was a considerable feat. Toward nightfall, they came to a cabin on Camas Prairie and found a crust of bread, so hard, the Indians had left it. He soaked it in spring water and let Maggie eat some of it. This differs from the version in which he found

Figure 4.11 A fanciful depiction of Pat Brice being confronted by Nez Perce men as he carried Maggie Manuel to safety. The pack to hold Maggie was not made until the next day. The Nez Perce did not dress like apaches, and the cross tattoo on his chest is a silly myth. The drawing was originally published in the memoirs of Colonel George Hunter. Hunter, George, "Reminiscences of an Old Timer: A Recital of the Actual Events, Incidents, Trials, Hardships, Vicissitudes, Adventures, Perils, and Escapes of a Pioneer, Hunter, Miner, and Scout of the Pacific Northwest, Together with his Later Experiences in Official and Business Capacities ... The Several Indian Wars, Anecdotes, etc." Battle Creek, Michigan: Review and Herald, 1889.

enough to cook a meal. He made a device to carry Maggie on his back and walked on the next day past bodies and burned out ruins. He staggered on until he saw Mount Idaho on the evening of Monday, June 18.[57] The citizens sent out a delegation that took Maggie from him, and one of them gave Brice a Prince Albert coat to cover himself. Mrs. Lyons set Maggie's arm, and both these survivors were well fed. George Popham was there already, he claimed, and he took care of Maggie for a while. This was untrue; Popham did not arrive at Mount Idaho until Tuesday evening a full day later than Brice and Maggie.

All accounts agree that the Manuel house was burned Sunday morning, June 17. The details of how and why remain elusive. Jeanette and her son were never again seen after that Saturday night. The mystery of her disappearance remains to the present day.[58]

Explanations of the Jeanette Manuel Mystery

Here, I can summarize the various proposed explanations about Jeanette's fate and the sources of each:

1. H. W. Cone, Slate Creek store owner, said he heard Indians say a drunken warrior killed her.

2. Poe and Brown claimed to find human bone in the Manuel house ashes but Chapman said the bones were not human. If the presence of human bone could be irrefutably established this would end the question. Mr. Conley who was the first at the fire scene, and who was seconded by George Riebold, found no evidence of a body. His report seemed the most solid. Others talk of animal bone being present. Poe and Brown may have mistaken these for human bone.

3. Red Wolf said she died from the initial fall from the horse, but possibly was taken back to her house "before life entirely departed."[59] This is vague and self-contradictory. Jefferson Green (Black Feather) blamed a fall from Red Wolf's horse for the death also. The timetable for these events was vague. Norman Adkinson related tales of her being buried by Nez Perce women after she was killed in some unknown event. This would explain the reason her body was never found.

4. In 1900, Yellow Bull said she disappeared, presumably murdered, on Lolo Pass after two men quarreled over her. She would have been a captive many days, traveling over very rough ground with her injured knee, and near to several battles for this to be true. It fails to explain the whereabouts of little John, Jr.

5. In 1935, Peo-Peo Tahlikt also said she was killed on Lolo pass but added Joseph himself took her scalp. The abduction stories are supported by vague reports from "squaws" at the time that she was a prisoner. During this 1935 time period, there was much argument among treaty and Non-treaty Nez Perce about the role of Joseph in their history. He may have been named just to damage his reputation. Also, the trip up the Lolo Pass seemed too hard for her considering her injury, and the story still failed to explain John Jr.'s whereabouts.

6. John Miles (Weyah Wahsitskan) said she may have drowned in the Salmon—no one knows. Another report too vague to be of use.

7. Chapman said Indian women told him she was outraged by "the whole infernal outfit" and then wandered off and died. Chapman had a substantial and repeated problem with his veracity, and at one time or another supported many varying explanations. It is difficult to believe no one would have noticed where Jeanette wandered.

8. Maggie, with some support from J. M. Parsons, and particularly, yet only partially, from Duncan MacDonald, said Chief Joseph killed her at the Manuel home and she was burned to ashes in the house fire. Charlotte M. Kirkwood said that Jeanette's "underclothes and the baby's gown bearing the marks of the knife, were found hidden in the rocks."[60] This would support the idea that she was taken from her home during the night.

9. Mox Mox, in the Fall of 1877, told S. R. Matteer that he too had witnessed her death in the house fire. MacDonald said she was alive, not stabbed, when burned to death in the fire along with her infant.

10. A writer to the Walla Walla Union the following summer, 1878, said "Mr. Bloomer, of Mount Idaho, reports having seen a half-breed Indian who states that he has conversed with the wife of

Jack Manuel, and can prove it by half a dozen men, if he was not willing to take his word for it. Your readers will remember that Mrs. Manuel was reported captured and killed at the old Arthur Chapman place on White Bird. But it is now proved beyond doubt she is still in White Bird's camp alive." The Boise Statesman reprinted this under the headline, "Doubtful."[61] It is another version of the captivity story, but instead of dying in a quarrel she survived to go to Canada. Would she have been physically capable of the arduous journey? Would she never have had a chance to escape or alert the military during that long ordeal?

Of all the manifold accounts of the Manuel family tragedy in the many books on the Nez Perce War, McDermott's, *Forlorn Hope*, gives the best documented and best analyzed discussion of the possible explanations. As McDermott points out, Maggie said she and Brice returned to the house the next day after Maggie saw her mother there dead, but Brice saw the house empty—no body, no bloody floor. Earrings from the burned house, supposedly found near skull fragments, were kept by the Manuel daughters throughout their lives and are still extant. The burning of a half frame, and half log house would not totally consume a body. A great deal of bone and teeth would certainly remain and most likely some flesh. Deliberate cremations done with modern equipment inevitably leave about two to three pounds of bone fragments. Without a modern crematory a much greater volume is left. A fire that could not melt—in fact, scarcely damage—earrings could not vaporize a body.[62] The explanation of Jeanette's death remains as hidden as ever.

From Isabella's point-of-view, her husband, and best friend were both lost from her within two days of each other. She was no longer a wife, or a best friend, she was solely a mother; a mother with two small children to protect, as she headed up the impossibly steep trail toward Mount Idaho. Isabella was also walking into Idaho legend.

End Notes

[1] In the 1990s, the many mammoth skeletons excavated there attest to the age of Tolo Lake.

[2] Frances I. (Benedict) Shissler. *Bonners Ferry Herald*, Bonners Ferry, Idaho, 6 April 1939, p. 1, c.1 & 2, p. 6, c. 2 & 3. Frances was only eight at the time of the war, but present at these events and probably discussed them with her mother over the years. Her memoir is a valuable document.

[3] Frances I. (Benedict) Shissler. *Bonners Ferry Herald*, Bonners Ferry, Idaho, 6 April 1939, p. 1, c.1 & 2, p. 6, c. 2 & 3.

[4] Frances I. (Benedict) Shissler. *Bonners Ferry Herald*, Bonners Ferry, Idaho, 6 April 1939, p. 1, c.1 & 2, p. 6, c. 2 & 3.

[5] Wilfong, *Following the Nez Perce Trail*, p. 8, 78. There are numerous transliterations of the native names in different sources.

[6] McDermott, *Forlorn Hope*, p. 5.

[7] Sunrise on June 14 is at 4:54 a.m. and sunset is 8:43 p.m. PDT. Of course, few people of this day had watches, time zones were not yet invented, and neither was daylight savings time. What is applicable, is the fact that daylight lasted 11 minutes less than 16 hours. With twilight at sunrise and sunset, close to two more hours could be added to the long days less than a week from the summer solstice.

[8] Frances I. (Benedict) Shissler. *Bonners Ferry Herald*, Bonners Ferry, Idaho. 6 April 1939, p. 1, c.1& 2, p. 6, c. 2 & 3.

[9] Charlotte M. Kirkwood, *The Nez Perce Indian War Under War Chiefs Joseph and Whitebird*. Grangeville: *Idaho County Free Press*, p. 50. The account I present here combines the story as told by Isabella in Kirkwood's book and the version of Frances Shissler.

[10] Charlotte M. Kirkwood, *The Nez Perce Indian War Under War Chiefs Joseph and Whitebird*. Grangeville: *Idaho County Free Press*, p. 50.

[11] Frances I. (Benedict) Shissler. *Bonners Ferry Herald*, Bonners Ferry, Idaho. 6 April 1939, p. 1, c.1 & 2, p. 6, c. 2 & 3.

[12] Charlotte M. Kirkwood, *The Nez Perce Indian War Under War Chiefs Joseph and Whitebird*. Grangeville: *Idaho County Free Press*, p. 46. I have blended the two versions of the conversation as Kirkwood and Shissler reported them. They are substantially the same.

[13] Charlotte M. Kirkwood, *The Nez Perce Indian War Under War Chiefs Joseph and Whitebird*. Grangeville: *Idaho County Free Press*, p. 50.

[14] Charlotte M. Kirkwood, *The Nez Perce Indian War Under War Chiefs Joseph and Whitebird*. Grangeville: *Idaho County Free Press*, p. 47.

15 P. 77 of notes in file, unnamed author. If there was a Chinese cook, he disappeared after his first warning with no further mention.

16 P. 83, of notes unattributed. The Indians said they offered Bacon his life if he would come out but he refused to leave Benedict.

17 Frances I. (Benedict) Shissler. *Bonners Ferry Herald*, Bonners Ferry, Idaho, 6 April 1939, p. 1, c.1 & 2, p. 6, c. 2 & 3.

18 Charlotte M. Kirkwood, *The Nez Perce Indian War Under War Chiefs Joseph and Whitebird*. Grangeville: *Idaho County Free Press*, p. 50.

19 *The Teller*, Lewiston, Idaho, 7 July 1877, p. 1, c. 3-4.

20 It was still light when she reached the Manuel ranch three miles up the Creek from the Benedict store.

21 Charlotte M. Kirkwood, *The Nez Perce Indian War Under War Chiefs Joseph and Whitebird*. Grangeville: Idaho County Free Press, pp. 50-51. In this version, it is the next day when Isabella reached the Manuel ranch but this is unlikely.

22 Grant and Mary were in school at Mount Idaho along with Julia Manuel.

23 Isabella Benedict, Letter to Mrs. Orchard, and Mrs. Dougherty, her sisters. *Idaho World*, Idaho City, 13 July1877. Written at Mount Idaho on June 29.

24 McDermott, *Forlorn Hope*, p.18.

25 *Idaho Daily Statesman*, Boise, 3 Dec. 1911, p. 3, c. 1-5. Mrs. Walsh was with this party and told her story in the *Teller*, Lewiston 8 Sept. 1877, p. 3, c. 1-3.

26 Charlotte M. Kirkwood, *The Nez Perce Indian War Under War Chiefs Joseph and Whitebird*. Grangeville: *Idaho County Free Press*, p. 43. This entire paragraph is from this source. Helen Walsh also published a long letter in the Lewiston newspaper at the end of August giving the details of that day. See *The Teller*, Lewiston, Idaho, 8 September 1877, p. 2, c. 1-3.

27 Frances I. (Benedict) Shissler. *Bonners Ferry Herald*, Bonners Ferry, Idaho. 6 April 1939, p. 1, c.1& 2, p. 6, c. 2 & 3.

28 Isabella Benedict, *Idaho World*, 13 July 1877. Written at Mount Idaho 29 June.

29 Frances Shissler, "Story of an Indian Uprising," *Echoes of the Past*, p. 15. Frances I. (Benedict) Shissler. *Bonners Ferry Herald*, Bonners Ferry, Idaho. 6 April 1939, p. 1, c.1 & 2, p. 6, c. 2 & 3.

30 The facts of the events at the Manuel ranch could never meet a legal test of "beyond a reasonable doubt," however a "preponderance of evidence" test might be possible. Human memories were all sightly different.

31 Adkison, J. Loyal. "Benedict Family Closely Related to Early Idaho History," *Idaho County Free Press*, Grangeville, Idaho, 27 March 1952.

[32] Wilfong, *Following the Nez Perce Trail, : A Guide to the Nee-Me-Poo National Historical Trail with Eyewitness Accounts.* Eugene: Oregon State University Press, 1990. pp. 79-80.

[33] Wilfong, *Following the Nez Perce Trail,* p. 86. The Benedict children were seven year-old Frances (Frances) and one-and-a-half year-old Addie. See Obituary of Addie Benedict Brown, age 89 (sic), *The Florence Miner,* 8 January 1898, p. 3, c. 2-4. Robie was one of the men who furnished lumber (at $70 per thousand feet) to build Fort Lapwai. *Idaho Daily Statesman,* 21 November 1909, Section II, p. 5, c. 4-6.

[34] Frances I. (Benedict) Shissler. *Bonners Ferry Herald,* Bonners Ferry, Idaho, 6 April 1939, p. 1, c.1 & 2, p. 6, c. 2 & 3.

[35] Adkison, J. Loyal. "Benedict Family Closely Related to Early Idaho History," *Idaho County Free Press,* 27 March 1952.

[36] Duncan McDonald, "Goaded to the War-Path," *The New Northwest* (Deer Lodge, Montana) 21 June 1878, p. 2. McDermott, *Forlorn Hope,* p. 4n. A bit of the background of the author helps to explain his outlook and qualification for doing this research. See William S. Lewis, "Spent Boyhood Days at Old Fort Colville," *Spokesman-Review,* and William S. Lewis, "Indian Mounds of Spokane Country Unique: Angus Macdonald Told of Donation Feast Custom— Stories of long Ago," The *Spokesman-Review,* 19 September 1920, Section II, p. 2. Duncan's father Angus was the agent of the Hudson Bay Company at old Fort Colville from 1852-1871, and in all, spent 60 years trading with the north-west Indians. Duncan's mother was half Nez Perce and half French/Iroquois. He knew the Indians he was contacting.

[37] Laughy, Linwood. *In Puruit of the Nez Perces: The Nez Perce War of 1877 as Reported by Gen. O. O. Howard, Duncan McDonald,Chief Joseph.* Kooskia, Idaho: Mountain Meadow Press, 1993, p, 239-40. Duncan McDonald, "Goaded to the War-Path," *The New Northwest,* Deer Lodge, Montana, 21 June 1878, p. 2.

38 *The Teller,* Lewiston, Idaho 23 June 1877, p. 1, c. 3.

[39] *Eureka Daily Republican,* Eureka, Nevada, 29 June 1877, p. 3, c. 2 & 3.

[40] *The Teller,* Lewiston, Idaho, 30 June 1877, p. 3, c. 2.

[41] *Idaho Tri-Weekly Statesman,* Boise, Idaho, August 4, 1877, p. 2, c.3.

[42] Wilfong, Following the Nez Perce Trail, p. 80.

[43] Bailey, *River of No Return,* pp. 261-264.

[44] Fisher, "Nez Perce War," p. 31. Frederick "Patrick" Brice was born in Londonerry, Ireland, in 1837 and came to America in 1851. He went to Oregon and then to Idaho to search for gold. See McDermott, *Forlorn Hope,* p. 15.

[45] *East Washingtonian*, Pomeroy, Washington, Maggie's obituary, 14 April 1949, p. 1, c. 1-2.

[46] McWhorter, *Hear Me My Chiefs*, p. 216-7.

[47] Wilfong, *Following the Nez Perce Trail*, p. 80.

[48] McWhorter, *Hear Me My Chiefs*, p. 217.

[49] McWhorter, *Hear Me My Chiefs*, p. 218.

[50] McWhorter, *Hear me My Chiefs*, p. 218. The most preposterous retelling of the Brice legend, according to McDermott (p.105), was in March, 1911, issue of *Century Magazine*. This was also printed in the *Idaho Daily Statesman* (Section II, 5 March 1911, p. 7-8, c. 2-3.). Charles Stuart Moody said Brice offered to let the warriors do what they wanted to him if he could get the little girl to safety. Moody said Brice, true to his word, returned but the Nez Perce were so impressed they let him go. This article must bear a great deal of the blame for the errors in the legend that have persisted every since. Moody has Manuel's first name as James; he said Maggie lay in the brush three days with an arrow still in her arm, that Brice shot a chicken at the Manuel house and roasted it over the coals of the burning house, he said it was 50 miles from there to Mount Idaho; and that the pair encounter the Indians on the prairie and the Nez Perce let them go because the Blackrobes had taught them reverence for the cross. After reaching Mount Idaho safely, Brice returned to Chief Joseph who let him go and he went on toward Florence. This is quite a litany of imaginative fabrications.

[51] *Idaho Tri-Weekly Statesman*, Boise, Idaho, September 6, 1877, p. 3, c. 2.

[52] McDermott, *Forlorn Hope*, p. 106.

[53] A monument to the 33 men was erected at the Fort Walla Walla cemetery, and also there were monuments to the men who fell at Cottonwood Canyon. See *Idaho State Historical Society, Sixteenth Biennial Report*, 1938, p. 88.

[54] McDermott, *Forlorn Hope*, p. 106.

[55] *Idaho Tri-Weekly Statesman*, September 6, 1877, p.1, c. 3.

[56] John Hailey, *The History of Idaho*, 1910, pp. 322-325.

[57] Helen Howard said they made a circuitous route of 50 miles to get to Mount Idaho (*Saga of chief Joseph*, p. 157). This was not feasible nor would it have been helpful for concealment.

[58] See my book, *Jeanette Manuel, The Life and Legend of the Belle of Fabulous Florence*, 2009, for the most detailed explanation of Jeanette's disappearance.

[59] *The Teller*, Lewiston, 30 June 1877, p. 1, c. 3 & 4. The *Idaho World* of Idaho City (29 June 1877) mentioned Mrs. Manuel being burned in her house and remembered her as a former resident of their town. That would have been while married to Jacob Williams.

[60] Charlotte M. Kirkwood, *The Nez Perce Indian War Under War Chiefs Joseph and Whitebird*. Grangeville: *Idaho County Free Press*, p 48.

[61] Illustrated History of North Idaho, 1903.

[62] Ordinary house fires are usually 1200 degrees Fahrenheit or less. Complete cremation of a body takes one-and-a-half hours at 1600 to 1800 degrees and for an adult leaves two to three pounds of ash. See Swanson, Chamelin, and Territe, *Criminal Investigation*, 4th edition, (New York Random House, 1988).

5

MARY CAROLINE'S DIARY

1878-1880

IN JANUARY 1878, the new owner of the Manuel ranch, L. P. Brown built a building over the burned out ranch house and put a band of sheep on the range there.[1] The visible evidence of the Manuel residency along White Bird Creek was over. Jack and his daughters moved to Mount Idaho where he ran a saloon.

The Benedict family had an enormous adjustment to make also. Frances remembered this time: "After some months at Mount Idaho, we moved to Grangeville. Through the kindness of Mr. Crooks we were allowed to occupy the house near the Grangeville Mill built for the miller and his family."[2]

On Dec. 31, 1878, Isabella, 29-year-old widow with four children, paid Mr. and Mrs. Pearson $100 for lots 11, 12, 13, 14 of block five in Grangeville.[3] She had decided to run a rooming house—a very fitting profession for a widow with four children.

Following his rescue of Isabella and her children after the White Bird Battle, Ed Robie saw no further action in the war. He went into partnership with Peter Smith and they bought—for $850 in gold coin—the mining claims of the late James Baker, the elderly man who died trying to escape with the Manuel family. In 1878 and 1879 Robie and Smith worked these claims.

While living in Grangeville at the boarding house her mother opened, 13-year-old Mary Caroline "Carrie" or "Caddie" Benedict kept a diary.[4] It is an irreplaceable chronicle of those months.

Mary Caroline's Diary

2 AUGUST 1879, SATURDAY. Francis[5] and I went to Mrs. Johnson's[6] and stayed all night we had a good time and we went berring and got some berries in the evening we came home.

3 AUGUST, SUNDAY. I went to church this evening.

4 AUGUST, MONDAY. Mr. and Mrs. Flenner left this morning on the stage for Walla Walla and will remain a few weeks.

Borne

28 AUGUST, THURSDAY. Mrs. Hill had a little boy weighed 9 lbs.

Borne

29 AUGUST, FRIDAY. Mrs. McKinley has a pair of twins-a boy and a girl.[7] The girl weighed 8 ½ lb. and the boy 10.

Drowned

4 SEPTEMBER. 1879, Thursday. A school mate of mine Tomas Herman [Harmon?] he was dronded in the lake a swimming the men went out to hunt for him this evening.[8]

5 SEPTEMBER. FRIDAY. The men have not found him yet.

6 SEPTEMBER. SATURDAY. They are going to dive for him today.

7 SEPTEMBER. SUNDAY. Mr. Harris has dragged the lake and found him.[9] They will bury him as quick as they can.

8 SEPTEMBER. MONDAY. The ceremony was delivered at 11 o'clock I was not there because I did not know what time it was until it was over.[10]

9 SEPTEMBER, TUESDAY. I went up to Mr. Johnger this after noon the weather is very cold

10 SEPTEMBER, WEDNESDAY. Today is my 13 birthday. I had a present of a nice tie. The weather is cool. Mr. Bert Sherman is here he took dinner with us.[11] The Riebold girls & George was here.[12]

11 SEPTEMBER, THURSDAY. The weather is very fine. We washed to-day Miss Addie Pearson was here this after-noon and made a visit we combed your hair and made spit curls Had lots of fun.[13] Mr. Butler has just arrived from the wir bridge he has been driving pigs to the mines (Warrens) Mother is sick this evening and at supper Mr. Butler took sick not very much.[14] Brother got home from his work a few minutes ago.[15] Ed is up town at present my sister was not very well to-day neither.[16]

Figure 5.1 Portrait of Mary Caroline Benedict-"Carrie or Caddie" Benedict, the diarist of 1878-79. Photo from the collection of Deborah Starr.

A listing of marriages as recorded in the diary:

JULY 6 At the residence of the bride's parents by J. Boyers', Miss Susan Ruby to Mr. R. M. G. Bradley all of Grangeville.[17]

AUG. 11 By Rev. J. T. Flenner Mr. M. P. Crooks to Miss Mary Behean all of Grangeville, I. T.[18]

4 DEC., At Mount Idaho by J. Bowers Mr. T. B. Butter to Miss C. Riebold.[19]

A listing of Births as recorded in the diary:

SEP. 15, Grangeville, I. T. Mr. and Mrs. Crane a son weighed 8 lb.[20]

SEP. 30, Grangeville, I. T. Wife of C. Day a daughter 8 lb.[21]

OCT. 9, Grangeville, I. T. Wife of Hiram Titman a girl 12 pounds.[22]

JAN 20, About 6? Miles from to the wife of D. Telcher, a girl.[23]

MARCH, In this place on the 10th to the wife of W. C. Pearson a son weighed 9 lb.[24]

12 SEPTEMBER, FRIDAY. Very fine day. Mrs. Susan Bradley was here this afternoon and made a short visit. Miss Maggie Robinson Called this evening.[25] Mother washed some flannel shirts this afternoon. Brother got home from working with the thrashing machine. Mrs. Smith is sick again.

13 SEPTEMBER, SATURDAY. The weather was very fine. Dr. Morris walked to see Boney Malery[26] Francis and I cleaned the house all up. Mrs. Wicklow arrived from the river.[27] This evening she and Mrs. Crooks called a few minutes this evening[28] Mr. Earl came up also with a load of fruit Butter and Ed stacked mother hay this morning[29] Mrs. Riebold was a few minutes we tied a comforter this after noon.

14 SEPTEMBER, SUNDAY. I went to Sunday school this morning

Our pastor Mr. Haul has arrived.[30] Mr. Shisler[31] and Susie and Mrs. Shearer was here all took dinner with us[32] Mr. Rochphere also was here.[33] Miss Riebold and Lizzie was here and Mr. Large[34] this evening Mr. Hughes was here.

15 SEPTEMBER, MONDAY. I was sick today Mrs. Yane made a fashionable call.[35] Mr. McNeir is hauling mothers lumber[36] Mr. Butler went to his ranch to look for water but did not find any. A large fire can be seen on the prairie. Mrs. Wilkton? Left this morning for La Grande to teach school.[37] Mr. Gibbons and Joe arrived from Salmon river this afternoon with vegetables for us and some melons. Dr. Morris was here to see Bony. I finished the book Derby Haven Mr. Markham and Harry Called this evening[38] mother was called away to see Mrs. Crane

16 SEPTEMBER, TUESDAY. I washed today Miss Gussie Reinheart and Addie Pearson was here a few minutes.[39] Mr. Butler has gone to his ranch this morning to dig for water Miss Gussie and Miss Pearson is going to start for the river this after noon Mr. Large left for the river this morning Mr. Riggins is sick.[40] Allie is going to stay all night with me Mrs. Smith called a few minutes this evening I saw Mrs. Cranes little baby

17 SEPTEMBER, WEDNESDAY. Allie Riggins has gone home Mr. Markham and Mr. Carpinter went to the river this morning.[41] Francis and I mopped the floor this morning. Mother went to Mrs. Crane.[42] Mr. Jack Butter made a short call this morning. Mr. Robinson and Mr. Haul called this morning. Mr. Crofford took supper with us. Mr. Joel is going to stay with bony all night.[43] Mr. Haul and wife moved from Mr. Robinsons to Mrs. Rices house.[44] I called on Mrs. Rauch.[45]

18 SEPTEMBER, THURSDAY. Francis and I ironed this morning Ed went down to get Mrs. Caimbridge to stay with Mrs. Crane.[46] Mother went up a moment to see Mrs. Crane. Mr. Butter called a few minutes. Mrs. Crofford took supper with us.

19 SEPTEMBER, FRIDAY. I am going to stay with Mrs. Crane to-night.

20 SEPTEMBER, SATURDAY. I am staying with Ms. Crane.
Mr. Crane had breakfast at half-past (?) this morning an old
acquaintance of mine came to see Mrs. Crane this morning
It was Willie Anderson from Lewiston Mrs. King and Mrs.
Crooks, Julia and Margaret Manuel and Jessie King also Addie
Pearson was here and made short visit [47] Mr. Nathan Earl came
from the river today.

21 SEPTEMBER, SUNDAY. Frances and I went to Sunday school this
morning and church We also went to the funeral after church.[48]
Mr. Bert Sherman took supper with us this evening Ed McNeir
is not very well this evening.

22 SEPTEMBER, MONDAY. Mr. Tom Butter and Jack moved to
their ranch today to build a house. Mrs. Frances Yates made a
short visit this evening[49] I and Frances went to Mrs. Crooks'es
this evening[50] I met Mr. Foss this evening Mother bought 50?
Lb of pork today had a very big washing Mr. Anderson visited
us to-day Miss Gussie called this morning.

23 SEPTEMBER, TUESDAY. Mr. B Sherman took dinner with us
I scrubbed today. I went to Singing school this evening They
moved Mrs. Crane to Mrs. Bradley's[51] I have her bird to take
care of. Mrs. Caimbridge is waiting on her I called to Mrs.
Smith[52] Ed came to see us this evening. Dr. Morris was married
to Lewiston today.[53]

25 SEPTEMBER. THURSDAY. Dr. Morris arrived from Lewiston this
evening with his bride. Jim Crooks[54] arrived from Dayton with
his bride and sister Mr. and Mrs. Swarts and Peril (Pearl?) made
a short visit.[55] Mr. Crea called this evening.[56] Ed took supper
this evening. Mr. Earl made a fashionable call this afternoon
We ironed to-day Nelie Rauch came to get some flour[57]
Mr. Taylor went to Mr. Butter's to-day[58] The people are going
to shicer ree Jim to-night.[59] Brother is going with them

26 SEPTEMBER, FRIDAY. Miss Gussie Reinhardt called this morning Edward is working for Mr. Crooks. I called to Mrs. Rauchs' and also to Mrs. Bradleys I made Addie Pearson a visit this afternoon I went to practice to-day Mrs. Crane is worse Mrs. Blodget is waiting?[60] On her Mr. Earl and Mr. Ot from the river took supper with us Brother sent his name in the Red Cross about a week ago and to night is going in Mr. Smead was killed by the Indians a short time ago[61] About 130 soldiers arrived from the lower country Mr. Butter and Mr. Taylor is not very well Mother received a package from the east two white skirts Mr. Strong? Arrived from below

27 SEPTEMBER, SATURDAY. The weather is cool. Mr. Butter stayed all night. It rained all night. Mr. Ot went to town to-day[62] I went to Mrs. Yanes to visit her Mr. Taylor is not very well Mr. Pope spoke to me Mr. Rochephere called this evening Jim Crooks called this evening Frank Rauch called this afternoon. There was church at 11 o'clock I did not go

Figure. 5.2 Sunset on Camas Prairie. Storms and remarkable weather displays are common in this area. Photo by the author.

28 SEPTEMBER, SUNDAY It is raining and is very cold Mr Ot left
for the river I suppose he will get wet There is no Sunday school
today But church at Seven o'clock Mr. Rochphere was here
this evening Ed attended to Tom Clarks saloon to-day There
is church this evening brother is going but I am not going Mr.
Glinis? And another man came here to stay all night

29 SEPTEMBER, MONDAY. Mr Glinis is here Mr. Strong and Mr.
Haul called this afternoon Mr. Corn[63] also Mother and Francis
and I tied a quilt this after-noon Long? Bill took supper her
this evening. I Broke Mrs. Crane's bird cage the water cup The
weather is cool and blustering Ed went to the post today

30 SEPTEMBER, TUESDAY. We washed got done a little while ago
The wind is blowing and its raining Ed is not to home to-day Mr.
Brown[64] got hurt got his foot hurt a rassling with Mr. Crooks.
Brother is working for Mr. Crooks Mrs. Cambridge was to see
Mrs. Crane this after noon. We have a new boarder. Mr, Haul
came to get my Robinson Arithmetic Ed and Grant came home
this evening tired and wet. Ed has been to work for Mr. Crooks.

1 OCTOBER, 1879 WEDNESDAY. The weather is stormy and wet.
This fore-noon Ed cut some wood for Mr. Clark. Mrs. Rouch
called a few minutes this afternoon Mr. Earl brought mother
a box of peaches this morning. Francis and I slept in mothers
room. Mr. Pope gave me a paper of candy.[65] Mr. Rogers came
here this evening will stay all night.[66]

2 OCTOBER, THURSDAY Ed is working for Mr. Crooks and Grant
also I scrubbed the house Mr Victor a friend of ours from the river
called this after-noon Francis and Addie went to see Mrs. Rauch
this after noon I got some calico to line my quilt Mother went to
see Mrs. Crane this evening Mr. Coon came home with mother
Brother went to singing this evening Francis and I didn't go.

3 OCTOBER, FRIDAY Miss Gussie Reinhardt called this morning.
Mother put my quilt in the fraim. Mother went to town with

Mr. Brown and got me the first pair of corsets and two side dishes and some flannel, a belt ribbon, some calico. Mr. Bradley came for some light-bread for Mrs. Crane. Brother went to Red Cross. Mother is not very well this evening.

4 OCTOBER, SATURDAY. I scrubbed this morning. I brought Mrs. Yane some (?) yeast. Mrs. Rouch called this morning. Mr. J. Butler came to get the pitch fork.[67] I went to see Mrs. Hall this afternoon and also went to the bucher shop for some meat Mr. Taylor went to town. Just got home from work Mr. Rogers came here this evening Ed stopped in a minute he was in a hurry to go to his work and would not stay Mr. Rhett[68] broke jail the night before last and came over here and talked with Mrs. Crooks and Mike He was in prison at Mount Idaho Francis and Addie went to see Addie Pearson[69] I put on my corset this after noon for the fist time they fit splendid Mr. Rogers stayed all night lat night he came here after we had all gone to bed

5 OCTOBER, SUNDAY. I went to Sunday school and also Francis Mr. Robinson came to see if he could get Ed to work for him I don't know if he did or not Miss Gussie and Miss Alma Markham called this morning.[70] Mr. Hughes called this afternoon. Charles Cone an old friend from Salmon River also … Mr. Chamberlin made a short visit.[71] I went home with Alma and she and I came up and went to church together. Mr. Rochphere and Charles Cone and Francis and Grant also went Mr. Cone stayed al night. Brother went home with Alma after church. The weather cold it snowed last night on the mountains. The Gibbons from Salmon river stayed all night.

6 OCTOBER, MONDAY. Poe from Salmon river took supper here this evening. Also Frank Rauch got his arm broken he had it broken 5 weeks ago and was just getting well so he could use it. And this after-noon he jumped from a plat-form at the mill and broke it again The weather is cold. Mrs. Susan Bradley called a few minutes. Mrs. Crane called a few minutes this after noon.[72]

7 OCTOBER, TUESDAY. Mrs. Moley Chapman and Maggie was here to-day and took dinner with us.[73] It is the first time we have saw her for six years Miss Francis Yates called this afternoon. Brother and Charles Cone and Mr. Ot and Mr. Gibbons and Joe went to town. Mr. Ot and Joe had a lawsuit. Mr. Ot beat. Prof Plummer from below arrived on the stage this evening and is stopping here. He will give one of his evening entertainments to-morrow I think.

8 OCTOBER, WEDNESDAY. We washed to-day Mrs. Rauch and family came here to-day. Mrs. Rauch quilted on my quilt. Mrs. Hill and Aggie and baby called this evening[74] Mr. Caner? Took dinner with us to-day Mr. Jake Rievley? Came here for dinner this after noon Mr. Crane came here this afternoon after mother Mrs. Crane sent after her Prof. Plummer has gone to Mount Idaho to give one of his entertainments Mr. Gordon called on business this morning[75] Today is Ed's 21 birthday[76] Mr. Martin and Mrs. Martin and children arrived from Lewiston to make a visit at her Mothers for a month or so[77] Mrs. Susan Bradley called this evening

9 OCTOBER, THURSDAY. Today is Francis and Grant's birthday.[78] Grant is 15 and Francis is 11 Brother had a present of some candy and so did Sister

She also had a present of a pair of kid gloves and a bottle of pickles Mr. Rochphere took dinner with us Mr. Crea called a few minutes and also Mr. Rogers There is singing this evening and also teachers meeting I and Francis did not go Brother went Brother bought some butter to-day Mr. Jim Fallom took dinner with us [79] The weather is cold and wet

10 OCTOBER, FRIDAY. Ed came here this morning before breakfast. L. L. Gordon called this morning a few minutes[80] Mr. Taylor went up to the mountains this morning to cut wood Packed his blankets Mr. Brown came from Mr. Butter's this evening he

has been five hours on the road Brother went to Red Cross this evening I went to see Mrs. Crane and Susan Bradley to-day The weather is just like winter it snowed and hailed this afternoon Mrs. Blodget made us a visit Francis has a sore eye I finished an undergarment Mr. Fallom was here to-day he went to Mr. Earn Smith's this evening[81] Francis scrubbed the kitchen and pantry this afternoon.

11 OCTOBER, SATURDAY. I ironed this morning Miss Maggie Robinson called The weather is cold Charley Coon was here and made a short visit[82] I finished an undergarment this evening Mr. Rochphere was here Mother finished my quilt.

12 OCTOBER, SUNDAY. Francis and Grant and I went to Sabbath school The Stage came this morning the horses ran away Mr. Crofford was kicked on the head and in his breast Mr. Eastman the driver was not heart[83] he picked Mr. Crofford up and packed him a mile to Mr. Ramb's? Mr. Crofford was knocked senseless Mr. Crofford was here for supper I met Mr. Conover he also was here for supper Mr. Crooks was here this afternoon We received a letter from Mr. Holmes he got home all safe Mother sent a letter to Mr. Dorland ? of Cal I also sent a letter to Mr. Holmes in answer to the one I got from him Mr. Crofford will stay here tonight. Mr ?? came here this evening. He is not very well he has the sick headache.

13 OCTOBER, MONDAY. We washed to-day The weather is cold and rainie Mr. Baly Chamberlin took dinner with us to-day[84] Miss Gussie Rheinhardt called this morning Jake Hicks came from Mr. Joh Adkinson to-day Mr. Jude Crofford went to Lewiston.

14 OCTOBER, TUESDAY. I went to see Lizzie Riebold and Mrs. Titman's baby[85] Francis and Addie also went to see Mrs. Hill and Mrs. Crane Mr. Hall made a short visit Mother went to see Mrs. Crooks and Mrs. Pearson Mr. McNeir went to work for Mr. Robinson he is going to plow etc? Mr. Smith came from the

river this evening Mr Anderson came here to-day We all went
to the shoe this evening to Mr. Plummer we all got bilked I met
Mrs. Williams[86] Mrs. Crea and Charley Crooks left this
morning on the stage for Iowa

15 OCTOBER, WEDNESDAY. We ironed to-day I took sick this
fore noon Mrs. Hall made a visit this after noon Mr. Cone can
Indian Joe came from the river Mr. Rochphere was her to-day

16 OCTOBER, THURSDAY. Mrs. Bradley was here Mr. Smith went
to the river I went to see John Crea he is very sick Brother and
Charley Cone went to the dance and there were not many
there were 8 tickets sold only 8 ladies there Edward was here
this evening and stayed a while Charley Cone and Joe started
for the river this morning and also Mr. Anderso Brother went
to Red cross this evening Perry Sherman was here this evening
Mr. Brown went after the Dr. for John Crea I went to see Mrs.
Crane and Mrs. Yane Mrs. Shissler and Annie was here Mother
made some tomatoes preserves this after noon Lee Smith is sick
Minnie Rice came and brought our peleater? home[87]

18 OCTOBER, SATURDAY. We mopped Jake Hicks helped us We
got a load of wood from Mr. Hughes We went to practice this
afternoon Mrs. Jordan and Mrs. Crooks was here this afternoon[88] Bert and Perry Sherman was here

19 OCTOBER, SUNDAY. We went to Sunday school Brother and the
Sherman boys went Ed was here this morning I have got a new
hat Mrs. Rauch was here We all went to see Mrs. Carpenter[89]
and Mrs. Bradley also Mrs. Crane

20 OCTOBER, MONDAY. We washed today Charley Case was here[90]
We all went to Prof. Carry's entertainment Charley Rochphere
was here

21 OCTOBER, TUESDAY. We ironed to-day Mr. Woods and Charley White came from Slate Creek[91] Mr. and Mrs. Rauch and
Frank was here

22 OCTOBER, WEDNESDAY. Mr. Woods and Charley White went to Mount Idaho to-day Mrs. Ra (uch) was here

23 OCTOBER, THURSDAY. Addie Pearson and Katie and I went to Maggie Robinsons We had a good time Brother Butter was here[92] Charley White went to cotton wood to take a ranch We went to singing this evening

24 OCTOBER, FRIDAY. Charley White came from Cotton wood this evening

25 OCTOBER, SATURDAY. Jake Hicks went to Lewiston Charley White and Grandpa went to the river[93] Mr. Brown went to Clearwater We Mopped the house George Riggins was here[94]

26 OCTOBER, SUNDAY. We went to Sabbath school and churches. We got our prizes Mr. Eurich was here[95] Mr. Taylor Joe Mr. Gibbons Joe's Son Mr Smith Edward ? and Mr, McNeir called this evening Mother went to see Mrs Rauch Thurston Roby came to get my saddle?[96]

27 OCTOBER, MONDAY. We washed Mrs Yane was here Jim Fallon came here We went to practice but? Gussie had the Organ? All to pieces I helped her clean? It and also Francis Griff Roberts came from the river[97] Mr Brown came from Clear Water. Gussie Addie and Alice dressed? In men's clothes and went around town

28 OCTOBER, TUESDAY. We ironed Jim Fallon went to Benoys to work Charley Rochphere was here Tommy Aram came here to get Jim[98] Charley R. brought the mail We got cousins Christor? And Bertie? And Jessie' picture. Mr. Eruich was here Mrs. Yane and Mrs. Rauch was here We got a letter from Aunt Mary and Aunt Sarah

29 OCTOBER, WEDNESDAY. Mrs. Jones and Mr. Martin was here & Griff came from town Mother mopped We all went to the show??

30 OCTOBER, THURSDAY. Griff went to the river Grant and Mr. Anderson came from the river[99] John crea was here Mrs Rauch was here Jake came from Lewiston the weather is cool Grant went to singing

31 OCTOBER, FRIDAY. The weather is cool We received a letter from Aunt Mary also got her picture Mother finished my dress I went to Addie's this after-noon. Bill Anderson went to town Berk was here to-day Grant and Jake went a hunting[100] Jake painted the cupboard and the table legs Mrs. Haul moved today.

1 NOVEMBER 1879, SATURDAY. We mopped today Mrs. Rauch was here. We went to practice Jack Butler took supper with us Mrs. Rice moved to town this morning

2 NOVEMBER, SUNDAY. We went to Mrs. Hills to-day We went to Sunday school. The weather is fine The Red Cross marched and erected the tomb Stone on Charley Huston's grave[101] Mr. Rochphere Jack Butter and Mr. Bushay took dinner with us to-day Edward was here this evening and took supper with us. Grant Jack Riley Mr. Jordan Brown Edward McNeir all went to church Mr. Robie came from Salmon river to-day Francis and Addie and I went to Mrs. Crooks' and Mrs. Yane's to-day Mrs Yane and Mr. went to Lewiston Mother went to Mrs. Rauch's today We went to see then erect the tomb Stone

3 NOVEMBER, MONDAY. We all went to school the first day of the fall term Mrs Robie went to town today[102] Mr. Howard came from the river today[103] Mr. Bush is here Addie had a present of a doll for a birthday Mother got a letter from Lewiston

4 NOVEMBER, TUESDAY. Today is Addies 4th birthday[104] The funeral was largely attended service in the hall at 10 o'clock[105] Mr. Carry was here to bye our place Mrs. Crooks was here this evening We are getting along nicely at school Mr. Brown went to Mr. Reynolds Gussie and Mrs. Pearson went to visiting this Grant drove the bucher wagon down to Jim's?? Mr. Alexande

came upon the stage the eavening Mr. Eruric called this eavening Frances Yates took dinner with us to-day[106]

5   NOVEMBER, WEDNESDAY. Addie and Tom Pearson came to school [107] Alice Crooks also We have a very good teacher The weather is cold Mother washed to-day Mother got a letter from a friend in Cal stated that her husband was dead his name was Henry Dorland? Alice and J (ink blot) Crooks was here this evening[108] Nellie ran off and Alice came after her[109] she was told by her parents to go home and did not Gussie give lessons to-day I took a lesson Joe and Mr. Gibbins was here

6   NOVEMBER, THURSDAY. Bert and Pery came from the river today Mr Alexander took supper with us this evening[110] Joe and Mr. Gibbins also was here The weather is cold and it snowed some this afternoon Jerome and Miss Rice was here to-day

7   NOVEMBER, FRIDAY. John Carry was here this morning Bert and Perry was also here Harry Cone came from the River Grant and Harry went to red Cross this evening I had a very good music lesson I saw Ed to-day Jake went to Earn Smith's to-day The weather is cold Bill Darrah came here and bill Anderson came from the river

8   NOVEMBER, SATURDAY. We ironed a few things and also moped Mrs. Rauch and Mrs. Grear was here Mr. Livingston the peddler came here this evening Grant went to Mt Idaho lodge and also Harry Cone I went to practice Mrs. Hall Miss Gussie Reinhardt and Addie Pearson cleaned the hall Mother bought some thins of the peddler

9   NOVEMBER, SUNDAY. We went to Sabbath and church Francis and I went to see Mrs. Markhams folks Charley Rochphere was here The weather is cold

10   NOVEMBER, MONDAY. We washed to-day a new scholar came to school

11   NOVEMBER, TUESDAY. Miss Gussie give music lessons today

12 NOVEMBER, WEDNESDAY. (No entry)

13 NOVEMBER, THURSDAY. Mr. Fell Helmore[111] and Joe and
Johney Gibbson came from Salmon River today?

14 NOVEMBER, FRIDAY. Mrs. Caimbrige and Mr. Caimbrige and
Johnny Byrom Tom Butter also Geo Hashegan here Bill Anderson came here for dinner The weather is cold I joined the Red
Cross to night Dick Adkinson was here Mr. Benson raise quite
an excitement

15 NOVEMBER, SATURDAY. We scrubbed today Mr. Markham
took dinner with us Mr. Morks? And I bought some things of
the peddler also mother.[112] Francis and I went to practice the
weather is unpleasant Geo Hashigan is boarding here and
Mr. Nugent[113]

16 NOVEMBER, SUNDAY. We went to Sunday school to-day Francis
got two prizes at Sabbath school to-day for verces Mr. and Mrs.
Rauch was here and Susan Bradley Mr. Euric was here also
Edward McNeir was here a few minutes he came to bring Mr.
Robie a letter Edwards brother came up from Lewiston a few
days ago he is now working at the Hotel for Mr. Titman Alice
Riggins was at Sabbath school today[114]

17 NOVEMBER, MONDAY. We washed today Three new scholars
came to school to-day Mrs. Susan Bradley as here this after
noon John Crea is here at present Mr. Pope gave me one of his
pictures Mr. Livingston the peddler gave me a back comb and
some beads he went to Lewiston to-day Charley Coon came
from Lewiston on the stage this evening

18 NOVEMBER, TUESDAY. We went to school I took my music
lesson I had an invitation to the Grange's harvest feast
Mr. Eruic was here this evening

19 NOVEMBER, WEDNESDAY. Leroy Gordon[115] was here and also
John Crea Miss Susan Markham was here

20 November, Thursday. Mr. Eruic was here Mother went to Mrs. Crane and Mrs. Yane.

21 November, Friday. George and Mr. Radie was here Mr. Brown Came from Mr. Swars to-day Tomas Pearson E. P. Elmin? And Mr. Roberts joined the Red Cross this evening (??I washed to-day??)

22 November, Saturday. We scrubbed to-day Mr. Swartz was here to-day Mr. Nugent went to the red Cross at Mount Idaho We all went to the harvest feast at the Hall I spent a pleasant evening all was pleased.

23 November, Sunday. We went to Sunday school Mother went to church I got (dinner?) to-day. Mother Francis and I went to Mrs. Hills and had a very pleasant time. I saw Edward and his brother but no to speak to them. I went by and got Lizzie Riebold to go to Sunday school. Mr. Serge?[116] And Mr. Coresh? Took supper with us this evening. He has not been here for very near a year before it. Grant went to church this evening Mr. Eruic is here at present Mr. George Shearer was here this morning.

24 November, Monday. We washed Mr. Robie went to town. Leroy Gotrdon was here. Fred Shissler took dinner with us Harry George Shearer? Was here also ???? afternoon Mr. ???? this evening. (this entry not readable)

25 November, Tuesday. Mrs. Eckles took dinner with us today.[117] Mother bought some apples from Mr. Mortin?

26 November, Wednesday. [Isabella's 31st birthday] Mr. Robie commenced to oil? The house John Crea was here this morning to-day is mother's birthday[118] Tom made her a present of a set of colars and cuffs.

27 November, Thursday. Mrs. Swarts[119] Dela and Birdie also Robert Neugent was here on their way to the party at Mount Idaho Mother bought some Corn Meal Jake came from Mrs.

Morrises this morning. Grant and Addie, tom Pearson and I went to Maggie Robinsons Lizzie Leroy George also was there Maggie gave a Thanksgiving dinner for her Sabbath school class We spent a very pleasant Evening Mr. Euric was here Mr. Large came from Mount Idaho here to-day Addie fell in the fire place but did not get out before the fire had to burn her She also went to lift a chare and the back came of.

28 NOVEMBER, FRIDAY. Mr. Watson and Mr. Bushay was here for dinner Grant went to Red Cross this evening I did not go Mr. Eruic was here this morning Addie and I went a sleigh riding with Mike at noon[120] Alice Crooks is sick The weather is cold and disagreeable

29 NOVEMBER, SATURDAY. We scrubbed today Mr. Sam Large went home this morning Jake Riley went to Mount Idaho Edward McNeir was here this evening. Francis and I went to practice Mrs. Rice was here. I went to Mrs. Crooks this evening to see Addie She has been sick Mr. Shumway came[121] Jim Chamberlin joined the Red cross[122] Francis went to Mrs. Yanes Mr. Smith was here Univercelest church this evening Mr. McAllister will preach

30 NOVEMBER, SUNDAY. Mrs. Mr. Chamberlin took supper with us[123] also Mr. Taylor Jack and Tom Butter also Edward took supper Mr. Harry Wolf[124] and Mr. Ot came here and Mr. Earl Lizzie Riebold was here Grant went to Mount Idaho after some nails and won an eleven dollar cordien for 50 cents. We went to Sabbath school this morning Mr. Dan Bowers was here and spent the evening[125] Mr. Joe Bowers a soldier was here and gave us some music on the cordien[126] we all spent a pleasant evening A man from Palouse came here he is selling chickens Mother got some from him Mr. Ulrich and Leroy Gordon was also here

1 DECEMBER, 1879. MONDAY. We washed Mother got her potatoes from Mr. Crooks Jake went to Cotton wood this morning

Mr. Dan Bowers was here this morning All the folks went to church this evening Charles Robinson came to school today

4 DECEMBER, THURSDAY. Mr. Samuel Milbourn and Mr. Charley White came from the river this after-noon[127] Mr. Urich and Mr. Jack Butler Mr and Mrs. Coon came from below to day We went to Mrrs. Yanes this evening and got acquainted with Mrs. Coon. We had a very good time.

5 DECEMBER, FRIDAY. Brother Tom was here. Mr. Taylor and Perry Sherman (Sherwin) was here Grant and I went to Lodge Mother ironed It snowed a little this after-noon.

6 DECEMBER, SATURDAY. Mr. Robie and Mr. Taylor went to Masonic Lodge this evening Jake Riley painted the sitting room to-day Francis and I went to practice to day We also scrubbed

7 DECEMBER, SUNDAY. Mrs. Rauch was here and George and Henryettie[128] John Crea and Urich Mr. Taylor and Jack Butter was here Mr. Edward McNeir and Mr. Rochphere and George Shearer also was here Charley White came from town Edward McNeir was here and Mr. Taylor and Jack Butter Mr. Robie also Mother and Addie went to church

8 DECEMBER, MONDAY. We washed to-day Jim Fallom was here Mr. Crooks and George Riggins also Mrs. Susan Bradley was here.

9 DECEMBER, TUESDAY. George Riggins ad Jack Butter was here Mr. Robie and Mr. Brown went to town this after-noon

11 DECEMBER, THURSDAY. August Pope and Mr. Jordan Brown went to Lewiston to-day Mr. Freinridge came to board with us to day[129] Jack Butter took dinner with us

12 DECEMBER, FRIDAY. Mr. Robert Nugent Jack is working for Dick Bradley and is boarding with us Jake Riley painted the sitting room Charley Coon Clyde Fountain and John Crea was here and spent the evening

13 DECEMBER, SATURDAY. No entry.

14 DECEMBER, SUNDAY. Clyde was here. Jake went to Mount Idaho Ed was here John Crea also was here We went to Sunday School this morning Mr. Fawny and Brother Tom was here[130]

15 DECEMBER, MONDAY. We washed. John Crea and Mr. Urich was here. Mrs. Rauch and Mrs. Crane and Mrs. Rice and Nettie and Gurty was here.[131]

17 DECEMBER, WEDNESDAY. Samuel Milbourn and Frank Strobe? went to town[132] Mr. Urich and John Crea was here Francis and Addie And myself went to see Mrs. Coon and spent a very pleasant hour Francis went to Mrs. Yane Mrs. And Mr. Swartz Called this evening.

18 DECEMBER, THURSDAY. Samuel came from town Edward hauled a load of wood Mr. Riggins Shisler and Bradley took dinner here to-day Brown arrived from below with some freight It snowed Mr. Butter Jack Riley and Grant went to writing school

20 DECEMBER, SATURDAY. We went to practice and we scrubbed to-day

21 DECEMBER, SUNDAY. George Riggins and Jack Butter went to Oro Fino this morning with some pigs We went to Sunday school Mr. Hughes was here.

22 DECEMBER, MONDAY. We washed The weather s cold Mother fell in the cellar and heart her foot

23 DECEMBER, TUESDAY. The weather is very cold Miss Gussie Reinhardt was here this evening I went to practice

24 DECEMBER, WEDNESDAY. Mr. Nuggent went to the party and Grant also Mrs. Rice got the supper The other men went and look on a little while.

25 DECEMBER, THURSDAY.[133] Mr. Ulrich, George,[134] Rochphere, Nugent, Milbourn, Robie, Smith, and Edward McNeir, Brown, Riley, Cone, Fredenridge was here for dinner. Edward Mr. Urich

spent the evening and Mr. George taught us how to dance some Clyde Fountain was here and Mr. Byrom this morning.

26 DECEMBER, FRIDAY. Mr. Coon was here and Mike Crooks. Mr. Milbourn got a Mr. Crooks sleigh and we went to Mr. Manuels and Mrs. Smith and we went to see Mrs. Eastman and Delia's also We had a very good time. Mrs Bradley was here Mr. Rochphere and Mr. Urich was here Edward McNeir also was here Mrs. Rauch was here

27 DECEMBER, SATURDAY. We scrubbed Mr. George brought us some presents I went to practice for the Consert a dance at Mr. John's school house this evening

28 DECEMBER, SUNDAY. Edward was here and Mr. Urich We went to Sunday School I went to Mr. Peatson's Mr. Hughes also was here Jake Riebold came from Warren's today.

29 DECEMBER, MONDAY. We washed Mr. George Foss was here and Mr. Joseph McNeir (Ed's brother).[135] We all went to the show this evening It was very good Miss Frances Yates called Jack Butter got home this evening

30 DECEMBER, TUESDAY. Mrs. Yane finished my dress. We practiced for the concert this after-noon. Mr. Urich was here and went to the concert with us, we had a very good time. There was a very good audience.

31 DECEMBER, WEDNESDAY. Mr. Foss and Mr. Joseph McNeir was here this they came before we got cleaned up. Mrs. Yane and Ora and John Crea and Mr. Urich was here Bob and Mrs. Rice went to the Ball at Mount Idaho[136] Robie and Grant finished the kitchen

1880

1 January, 1880. Thursday. Mr. Rochphere and Mr. Dick Roberts Mr. Hughes and Mr. Bradley was here Ed was here for supper and spent the evening Mother is not very well.

2   JANUARY, 1880. FRIDAY. Jake riley is working for Crooks. We
    tied a comforter for Mr. Woodward[137] Mr. Poe Mr. McNeir
    called this after-noon Grant and Frances is sick Clyde Fountain
    was here this evening We ironed this morning

3   JANUARY, SATURDAY. I scrubbed this morning Jake blackened
    the stove Earnest Pring was here for dinner[138] A party was given
    at Mrs. John Adkinson's Brother Jack went to see brother Tom
    to-day[139]

4   JANUARY, SUNDAY. I went to Sabbath school. The weather is
    very cold the snow is deep. Addie is sick. I went to see Alice
    Crooks this evening Mrs. Rice and Mrs. Bradley went also
    Mother went to Mrs. Yanes and to Mrs. Bradley's Mr. Urich
    was (here) this evening. Frances is not very well Clyde was here
    this evening also Mr. Robie put the picture up

5   JANUARY, MONDAY. We washed to-day I went to practice and
    to see Mrs. Hill Mr. Joel called this morning. (ink blot prob-
    ably says Addie) Addie is sick and Grant also Walter Fen is not
    expected to live[140] Mr. Urich is here at present and the folks are
    playing cards

6   JANUARY, TUESDAY. Grant is very sick and Frances is sick again
    The wind is blowing fearfully it blew the flame down this morn-
    ing Mr. Crooks and Mr. Hughes was here this after-noon Mrs.
    Rice was here evening Very near all people from here went to
    the Ball at camp Howard Mr. Urich John and Clyde was here

Figure 5.3 Early Grangeville street scene. Photo from the collection of Deborah Starr.

this after-noon Jake borrowed a paper from Ed's brother, the evening star. Jack went to town for the Dr. Samuel and I was playing fox and geese and I win every one played 10 games

7   JANUARY, WEDNESDAY. Dr. Morris was here this morning to see Grant and Frances and Addie.[141] The wind is blowing very hard. Mr. Robie and Jack and Mr. Urich is working on the flume. Clyde Fountain and John Crea Mr. Joel Mr. and Mrs. Caimbrige was here I win 5 games from Jack and 4 from Sam Berk went to town and back[142] Mr. Hughes

8   JANUARY, THURSDAY. Samuel Milbourn went to the river this morning Berk also went home Mr. Urich was here this Mr. and Mrs. Bradley and Miss Markham to see Grant I finished my apron Ed is here at present. He took supper with us this evening Grant got as letter from Willie Orchard I went to practice It snowed last night Mr. Hughes was here this evening Mr. Swarts took supper with us

9   JANUARY, FRIDAY. Mrs. Rice and Gurty was here Clyde and Mr. Fawny was here this morning I did not go to school this week I went to the store and got a pair of shoes I also went to Mrs. Rice's Jake painted the pantry The wind is blowing Jim Crooks was here this evening Mr. Crooks was here this morning to get Bob to go and hunt cattle for him.

10 JANUARY, SATURDAY. Mr. Shumway called this morning he was down and sit up with Mr. Markham last night[143] he has got a very sore hand he is out of his head all the time I mopped the sitting room and kitchen Francis scrubbed the pantry Mr. Hall and Mr. Williams was here this after-noon there will be a public installation in the grange this evening Jake Hicks went to town and got drunk[144] L. P. Brown hit him with a poker and cut a great gash in his head

11 JANUARY, SUNDAY. (unreadable copy) and Mr. Urich and Clyde was here Robie and Urich went to see Mr. Markham

12 JANUARY, MONDAY. We washed Grant and Francis went to school Addie Pearson is sick with the (ink blot) ndas.[145] Mr. Urich was here Jake painted the pantry.

13 JANUARY, TUESDAY. Mr. Brown and Mr. Crooks was here Jake is painting a checker board for Mr. Clark Bob and Joe McNeir hauled a load of hay Mrs. Susan Bradley was here I brought Mrs. Yanes baby carriage home form the hall Mrs. Swarts came up ad is at Mrs. Yanes Jack and Grant went to writing school.

14 JANUARY, WEDNESDAY. I went to see Addie Pearson Tom is sick also. Mr. Urich was here this evening

15 JANUARY, THURSDAY. Mr. Grear and Harry Cone came from Slate Creek Mr. Grear stopped off from the porch at Mr. Clarks and bruised his arm very bad it was dark and he could not see. Ed was here and spent the evening Edward and Mr. Brown and Jake and Grant had a game of whist.

16 JANUARY, FRIDAY. I went to Red Cross this evening Grant and Harry also went Bert and Perry Sherman (Sherwin) came from Lewiston this afternoon Mr. Jim Crooks and wife gave a candy pulling last night Mr. Crooks was here the weather has been very disagreeable the past? Few weeks

17 JANUARY, SATURDAY. Perry went to town this morning Bert and Pell went home this morning I scrubbed this morning Mr. Gordon was here this morning Nathan Earl and Mr. George Foss was here this evening We went to practice this afternoon

18 JANUARY, SUNDAY. Mr. Grear and Mr. Hughes and Mr. Foss was here this afternoon Mr. Grear took supper with us Mr. Urich was here this evening We all went to Sabbath school To-day and yesterday were beautiful the sun was so warm John Crooks came to see Harry to-day Clyde was here this morning Granbt Harry Jack and Robert Nugent went to church Francis Adddie and I went to see Mrs. Yane this afternoon Mr. Crooks was here this evening Bill Anderson came here this afternoon

He gave us a box of apples. Mr. Robie went to his ranch it was all there

19 JANUARY, MONDAY. Mother and I washed I went to see Mrs. Rauch this evening Jim Fallom was here Ella Fairfield came to school[146] Mrs. Emma Bence[147] Harry went to town Mrs. Gordon was here

20 JANUARY, TUESDAY. I went to Mr. Jim Crooks to see Addie Pearson I also took supper with them Clyde was here Mr. Brown and Jack a load of wood to Tom butter (or brother)[148] Mr. Markham came here this evening Jack and Grant went to writing school Addie Brown took first prize Dr. Morris was here for supper

21 JANUARY, WEDNESDAY. Mr. Binnard[149] Crooks, Talkinton,[150] Gordon Rochphere was here I did not go to school I was to Mrs. Rauch's Mr. Wells got on a wild horse and the horse fell on him and hurt him very bad Mrs. Yane and Mother went to see Mrs. White Jack Butter and Mr. Brown came back from Toms Fred Rice is very sick[151] Jack and Grant went to writing school

22 JANUARY, THURSDAY. Tom Pearson took first prize Jack butter second Bill schmadeki third in writing school[152]

23 JANUARY, FRIDAY. Miss Holahan[153] and Mrs Titman and Mr. Woodward and Beaum and Jim Crooks Jack Butter and Mr. Welch joined the Red Cross[154] Mrs. Hall Miss Gussie Reinhart and I played some music also Alice Crooks

24 JANUARY, SATURDAY. Harry and Charley Cone went to the River We scrubbed Mr. Hughes

25 JANUARY, SUNDAY. Sam Large and Clde and Mrs. Crane was here this afternoon Mrs. Crane and Edward was here for supper Ed did not stay long he was in a hurry Mr. Urich was here Grant went to the raffle

26 JANUARY, MONDAY. I went to the store and got some cotton flannel for mother Addie went with me

27 JANUARY, TUESDAY. Bob took Mr. Grear and Large to the foot
of the grade We washed Mr. Urich was here this evening
Mr. Large and George Grear wer on their way to Slate Creek
The weather is disagreeable

28 JANUARY, WEDNESDAY. The weather is disagreeable John
Crea was here this morning

29 JANUARY, THURSDAY. No entry

30 JANUARY, FRIDAY. Robert Nugent Jack Butter Grant and I
went to R. C. There were some? From Mount Idaho We had
a splendid time

31 JANUARY, SATURDAY. We scrubbed Jake Riebold is here I went
to practice Charley cone was here this morning

1 FEBRUARY, 1880, Sunday. We went to sunday school Tom
Aram Mr.Crooks and Jake Riebold was here this afternoon Jake
stayed here last night with Grabnt Edward came here this afternoon he spent the evening with us the men went to church

2 FEBRUARY, MONDAY. We washed I was to see Mrs. Hill and
Lizzie Mr. Brown went to work for Jake Crooks. Mr. Urich
went to clear Water. Rogers came here Mr. Johnston was here.

3 FEBRUARY, TUESDAY. Mr. Urich was here he got back from the
River to-day Joseph McNeir was here we thought he was goin
to stay for supper but he went when we did not know it bob
and Jack hauled some hay.

4 FEBRUARY, WEDNESDAY. Mr. Swarts was here bob and Jack
went to collect some money down on the other side of the
prairie charley White was here this evening Mr. Robie finished
my bedroom

5 FEBRUARY, THURSDAY. Charley White has taken the mumps[155]

6 FEBRUARY, FRIDAY. Miss Florence and Mary Yates was here
this morning they come down for to go with me to the Lodge
Jack and bob was to go along We started and Bob and Jack had

their overshoes to put on we told them to hurry up and we also waited for them was afraid we would be late and we off and left them.

7　FEBRUARY, SATURDAY. We scrubbed to day We went to practice and went to Mrs. Hills I took the mumps this afternoon[156]

8　FEBRUARY, SUNDAY. Mr. Urich was her for dinner Francis went to Sabbath School Mr. Webber was here for dinner[157] Mr. George Foss was riding a wild horse and he got throwed and the horse got away he then took Jack hores ad Bobs saddle to hunt for the hores and has not got back yet. Ed was here this morning and stayed all evening he and Addie played all evening she enjoyed it so much Charley Wilson came from the river this afternoon A box of apples was sent to me from Slate Creek. Jack—

9　FEBRUARY, MONDAY. Last night Mr. foss was out hunting for his hores and got off of Jacks horse to fix the saddle and he got away from (him) and he was left a foot

10　FEBRUARY, TUESDAY. Miss Reinhardt was here to see us She has taken the mumps[158] the weather is disagreeable Mr. Urich was here this evening

11　FEBRUARY, WEDNESDAY. Mother and Frances washed Mr. Robie went to Salmon River this morning Jack came from Tom's this morning but went back again Frankie was to Mrs. Halls

Figure 5.4 Grangeville in 1893. Photo from the collection of Deborah Starr.

12 FEBRUARY, THURSDAY. Mr. Darr from Genessee came here he is an old friend of ours.[159] He left here some two and a half years ago and he has come back for to buy som[160] get some horses from Mr. Crooks. Mr. Little was also here[161] Mr. Urich was here

13 FEBRUARY, FRIDAY. Grant went to Red Cross this evening John Crea and Mr. Hughes was here to-day

14 FEBRUARY, SATURDAY. John Crea was here Grant Mother Francis and Addie and myself got some valentines. Francis and I got two a piece. We went to practice.

15 FEBRUARY, SUNDAY. John Crea was here We went to Sabbath School Robert Nugent came from the river this morning It is storming fearfully this morning Mr. Crooks also was here this afternoon. Mr. Urich also was here

16 FEBRUARY, MONDAY. We washed Jack came from Toms Mr. Carry Mr. Otterson[162] Mr. Joe McNeir Mr. Coram was here this evening. We had a very good time Bob killed Rover.[163] I went to practice. It snowed today.

17 FEBRUARY, TUESDAY. Mr. Otterson and Joseph McNeir and Mrs. Rach[164] and family was here. Mr. Reynolds Jack went to Tom's this afternoon.

18 FEBRUARY, WEDNESDAY. Mr. Darr started for home this morning Mr. Ben Morris was here today[165] Mr. Large came from the river Mrs. Urich and Mr. James Carry also was here Again it snowed.

19 FEBRUARY, THURSDAY. Mr. Urich called this evening. Bob came Back from Mr. Swartz's to day We had such a good time at school today I got another valentine this morning

20 FEBRUARY, FRIDAY. Mrs. Rauch and her children and Mrs. Bradley was here this afternoon.

21 FEBRUARY, SATURDAY. (no entry)[unclear which day is missing]

22 FEBRUARY, SUNDAY. Mr. Rochphere and Mr. Hughes was here

this afternoon The weather is very fine Mother and Jasck Butter went buggie riding. Francis and I went to Mrs. Swarts with Robert Nugent. This evening Edward McNeir and Mr. Carey was here this evening.

23 FEBRUARY, MONDAY. Robert Nugent went to Mount Idaho on the ball Tom Butler was here We washed to day Jack took Brother Tom home and brought him back again The weather is very good

24 FEBRUARY, TUESDAY. Grant is very sick with the mumps.[166] Mrs. Rice was here this afternoon also Charley Robinson. I went to Episcopal service with Mrs. Rice. Jack and Bob went to church also.

25 FEBRUARY, WEDNESDAY. The weather is very cold Mr. Urich was here this evening. Dr. Nevis will preach at Mount Idaho this evening.

26 FEBRUARY, THURSDAY. Dr. Nevin held services here this evening Mr. Chapman came here this morning[167] We had not seen him since the spring of 77 he has been away.

27 FEBRUARY, FRIDAY. I went to Red Cross with Charley Robinson this evening Johney Byrom was here for supper and Mr. — Mr. Add Chapman came here to board.[168]

28 FEBRUARY, SATURDAY. Mrs. White called to see Grant also Mrs. Rauch and Mr. Urich I went to practice Mr. Rochphere was here I went to Mrs. Rauchs Brown went Mr. Jack Crooks Mr. Hughes was here

29 FEBRUARY, SUNDAY. Charley Rochphere and Charley Robinson was here this morning there was no Sabbath school this morning Mr. Carry was here this evening. I went to Mr. White's and Frankie went to Mrs. Yanes. Mr. Lain? Also was here the weather is very disagreeable

1 MARCH 1880, MONDAY. No entry.

Figure 5.5 Another scene of Grangeville. By this time Isabella had moved to the Robie ranch on Salmon River. Photo from the collection of Deborah Starr.

2   MARCH, TUESDAY. Chapman was here

3   MARCH, WEDNESDAY. Mr. Chaimberlain Tom Pearson and John Crooks was here this evening

4   MARCH, THURSDAY. I went to the store and to Mrs. Yanes Mr. Rochphere was here We all went to the Old Folks concert this evening John Crea and Mrs. Rice was here.

5   MARCH, FRIDAY. Addie Pearson has got the mumps[169] Mr. Hughes and Mr. Urich was here

6   MARCH, SATURDAY. We scrubbed Charley Rochphere was here We went to Practice the weather is very cold Mr. Hughes was I went to Mrs. Bradley and Mrs. Titmans. Her little baby has the mumps[170]

7   MARCH, SUNDAY. We went to Sabbath school Frankie went o Mrs. Yanes Edward McNeir spent the evening with us Mr. Smith and Mr. Rochphere and Mr. Urich was here this evening Robert Nugent went to Mr. Raney's place.[171]

8   MARCH, 1880, MONDAY. We washed bob came back from Mr. Raney' Miss Reinhardt and Mr. Rochphere was here Mr. Chapman went to Mount Idaho

[This is the end of Carrie's diary entries that were photo-copied—On April 19, 1880, about a month after the last entry, Carries' 32-year-old mother, Isabella (Kelly) Benedict, married Edward Robie at her home in Grangeville.]

End Notes

[1] *Tri-Weekly Statesman*, Boise, Idaho, 22 January 1878, p. 3, c. 4.

[2] Frances I. (Benedict) Shissler. *Bonners Ferry Herald*, Bonners Ferry, Idaho, 6 April 1939, p. 1, c.1 & 2, p. 6, c. 2 & 3.

[3] Idaho County Deed book. Some source say December 30.

[4] The diary was passed through the family for generations and was finally transcribed in 2004, Much of the original was faded and hard to read but it is a unique treasure in Idaho and Grangeville history. The diary is presented here as transcribed at that time. Most of the footnotes were made by the transcriber at that time. Spelling and punctuation have not been altered. It is sometimes hard to decipher. Mary Caroline was young with minimal time spent in school.

[5] Mary Caroline's sister Frances (Frankie), who would turn 11 in October.

[6] This could be Sarah (Wilmot) Johnson, wife of Henry C. Johnson.

[7] Nellie (Holohan) McKinley, wife of Alex D. McKinley. They have a 9-month-old girl, Mary, in the 1880 Census. (If twins, one died before 1880 Census) Also from 1880 Mortality Schedule we see that Nellie's father, Michael Holohan, age 46, had died of pneumonia in January of 1880. He left a wife Anna, 44, and large family of children, Peter, 23, Mary, 18, Michael, 16, Patrick W., 14, John, 8, and Anna, 6. Of these children, Mary Ann married Daniel Sebastian in 1881 and a P. J. (Peter?) married Mildren Sebastian, also in 1881.

[8] Probably Harmon—1880 Mortality Schedule: Thomas Harmoney, age 18, drowned September, resided in county three years, born in Kansas, his father in Kentucky and his mother in Pennsylvania. Thomas Harmon, Harmony, Herman is not reported buried in Idaho County cemeteries. His father John, widower, and a brother, Levi, 16, still reside in the area on the 1880 Census.

[9] John C. Harris, single, stockman, age 50 (1880 Census).

[10] The funeral ceremony of Thomas Harmon.

[11] Carrie consistently used "Sherman" but it is Sherwin who boards with them frequently.

[12] Riebold girls: Elizabeth was 14, Rosa, 9, Mary, 10, Catherine, 5, and George, 2,; children of Peter & Catherine Riebold (1880 Census). See p. 259 of *Idaho County Voices*.

[13] Addie Pearson—one of 7 children of Wm & Isabella Pearson, age 12 in June 1880 on the U.S. Census.

[14] Butler could be newly wed Thomas, age 30, or Jack, or Martin, 29, teacher. The wire bridge was an early river crossing on the Salmon River (River of No Return). "Mother" of course refers to Isabella.

[15] Brother must refer to Grant Benedict, the only son, He was about 14.

[16] "Ed" may refer to Edward Robie who married Isabella the following year.

[17] Actually John Bowers—he was a Justice of the Peace and Probate Judge of Idaho County. Susan Roby (Robie) and Richard Bradley, blacksmith, age 40 and Susan age 21 (1880 Census).

[18] P. 262 of *Idaho County Voices*, Rev. J. D. Flenner 'started' the Methodist Episcopal Church sent here by them. He started the private church school—Columbia River Academy. He was also a minister to the area. This is probably Michael Crooks, who married Mary A. Behan at the parsonage of Rev. J.D. Flenner. He was 28 and she was 17. Michael died about 30 September 1884; he is supposedly buried in Prairie View, but there is no marker and no record. Michael and Mary had two children, John M and Katie C. I. T. stands for Idaho Territory—Idaho was a decade away from statehood.

[19] In the 1880 Census, Thomas Butter (Butler) was 32 and Christina Riebold was 21. Butler is spelled both ways Butter and Butler—Its probably Butler—Thomas has a brother, Jack.

[20] Horatio and Adelle Crane. He was a saloon keeper; their son was named Albert.

[21] Cassius Day and his wife, Mary E; they named their daughter Bernice.

[22] Margaret Ella Turner, wife of Hiram Titman, married 1872; they named this daughter Edna.

[23] Diedrich Telcher and Margaret (Rauch). The child was named Margaret (1880 Census).

[24] William Pearson and Isabella Crooks Pearson. In the Census, June 11, 1880, the baby still had not been named, but in *Idaho County Voices*, p. 252, we see Ray D. was born in 1879.

[25] Maggie Robinson was 16 on the 1880 Census, daughter of James H. & Statira (deceased 1873) Robinson.

[26] Bony Mallory is on the 1880 Census Mortality Schedule. Bony may have been rooming with the Benedict family. He was about 37, male, white, single, miner, resided in county 10 years, and died from consumption. The doctor was J. B. Morris. The Mortality schedule said he died in August. The doctor must have made the entry from memory after the fact.

27 Rebecca E. Wilklow was 30 year old schoolteacher, a widow (1880 Census).

28 Mrs. Crooks could be Martha, age 58, wife of John M. Crooks or Victoria, 25, wife of Jacob W. or newlywed Mary, 17, wife of Michael, or Josie, 27, wife of James.

29 Probably Nathan Earl, age 41, dairyman, living with John and Mary Wood in 1880 Census.

30 William A. Hall, age 33, Methodist minister, who came to Grangeville in 1879 to take charge of Columbia River Conference Academy, also studied law. (See *History of North Idaho,* Western Publishing, 1903.)

31 Frank Shissler, age 40 and Susan, age 8.

32 Possibly Mrs. Susan Shearer, age 66, wife of Frederic.

33 This was most likely Charles de la Rochpierre, 24, single, a carpenter, native of Switzerland, who had arrived on Camas Prairie in 1878. He died in 1883 at the age of 29.

34 Samuel Large, rancher, who lived on Salmon River, age 39, on 1880 Census.

35 Mrs. Yane, mentioned often, was Matilda Giles, wife of Joseph Yane, who married on June 20, 1878 in Nez Perce County.

36 Two McNeirs: could be Edward, 20, or Joseph, 18 (1880 Census).

37 Possibly Wicklow, the teacher who returned by 1880 Census to teach in Grangeville area.

38 Either Nathan Markham, 50 or Frank, 23, Harry was 12 (1880 Census).

39 August Reinhardt, age 22, music teacher in 1880 Census. Addie Pearson later married (1888) Dr. Bibby, a local figure.

40 John T. Riggins, 35, was the father of Allie, 13, (1880 Census).

41 Augustus Carpenter, 34, whose wife was Mary, 26, (1880 Census).

42 Also on September 15 mother was called away to Mrs. Cranes. Adelle Crane, wife of Horatio, had a baby boy on 15 September. Mrs. Crane may have been ill following the birth as folks took turns staying at her home for several days.

43 Joel might be Joseph Jewell, 38-year-old herder (1880 Census). Boney Mallory is worsening and friends are staying with him until he dies.

44 Mrs. Rice: there are two Rice widows—Melissa and Hannah— who might presumably rent houses in 1880.

45 Probably Mary Rauch, 29, wife of John G., 39, wheelwright (1880 Census).

46 Mary Cambridge, 39, wife of Melton (1880 Census).

[47] Julia, 1, and Margaret, 8, were the daughters of Isabella's best friend Jeanette Manuel, Margaret (Maggie) had been injured when the Nez Perce conflict began. The family had moved to Mount Idaho. Jessie might be Josephine King, 13, daughter of Farrington B. and Harriet King.

[48] Must be the funeral of Boney Mallory, who died of consumption about this time.

[49] Daughter of William and Sarah Yates (age 14, in 1880).

[50] Mrs. Crooks could be Martha, age 58, Josie, age 27, or Victoria, age 25.

[51] Adelle Crane was apparently ill following the birth of her baby on September 15. Neighbors are taking turns with her for several days.

[52] Possibly Mattie Smith, wife of butcher George Smith.

[53] Dr. John B. Morris married Laura Billings on September 24, 1879, at Lewiston.

[54] James L. Crooks had married Josie Graham on September 18 in Columbia County, WA. James first married in Mount Idaho on Feb. 14, 1872 to L. J. M. (Lucy) Fields. Lucy died in 1873, probably at Nellie's birth. In the 1880 Census a school teacher, Augusta Rheinhardt, was boarding with them.

[55] Theodore Swarts and Electa (Lulu) Brown, and 1-year-old daughter, Pearl, (1880 Census).

[56] Crea could be James, 46, or John, 21 (1880 Census).

[57] This could be 10-year-old Melvina, daughter of John G. and Mary Rauch (1880 Census).

[58] Mr. Taylor could be one of the following: John, 57, retired miner; John H., 41, carpenter living with Peter Ready; Patten, 28, farmer; or Andrew Taylor, 45, miner in Elk City district (1880 Census).

[59] Shivaree—probably Jim Crooks and his wife.

[60] Asenath Blodgett, widow, age 63.

[61] Mr. Smead—If this refeers to A. D. (Pony) Smead, the information about his death was inaccurate. Pony Smead lived in the area, where from March to August 1879, there was Sheepeater fighting in the Salmon River. Three persons were reported killed, including Peter Dorsey, Hugh Johnson and James P. Rains. Mr. Smead was alive in 1880.

[62] Larry Ott lived on Salmon River, was reportedly involved in the starting of the War of 1877 as previously mentioned.

[63] Corn—no "Corn" in 1880 Census, but a Melzar Coon, and Charles and Henry Cone.

[64] Mr. Brown—could be either Chas. F. or L. P. Brown.

[65] August Pope was a local merchant (1880 Census).

[66] John Rogers, age, 42, born in Ireland (1880 Census).

[67] Joseph Butler, age 63, (1880 Census).

[68] Mr. Rhett—probably William Rhett.

[69] Mary Carolin's sister, Addie.

[70] Alma Markham was 19 in 1880, daughter of Nathaniel and Fannie Markham.

[71] Chamberlin could be James, 46, a butcher, Jerome, 21, James, 19, all single, (1880 Census).

[72] Adelle Crane must have finally recuperated.

[73] Molly Chapman and Maggie could be the Indian wife of Ad Chapman from Salmon River. They are not listed on the 1889 Census, but in 1870 Maggie was 5, so she would have been 15 at this time.

[74] Mary Hill (wife of William) and her daughter, Agnes, age 2 (1880 Census).

[75] A.H. Gordon, age 40.

[76] If this is Ed Robie, he would be closer to 41, not 21, so "Ed" may be someone else.

[77] There is a Mort and Jennie Martin in the 1880 Census. Mortimer Stiles Martin married Jane Freeman on June 12, 1877, just before the outbreak of the Nez Perce War.

[78] Francis and Grant were Carrie's siblings born on the same day, Grant in 1864 and Frances in 1868.

[79] This might be James Falloon, age 30, (1880 Census).

[80] L.L. Gordon, who was the 13-year-old brother of A. H. Gordon (1880 Census).

[81] Ernest Smith, age 47, (1880 Census).

[82] Probably Charley Cone, age 23.

[83] A Josiah Eastman married Mary J. Fountain in Nezperce County, on 17 November 1864. She has a son Clyde Fountain, 20, residing with them. Sadly, Clyde was killed by lightening while working on the range in Wyoming in August 1887. He was buried on the ranch there near the headwaters of the Bel Fourche River (newspaper items, 1886-1903).

[84] Jacob Bailey Chamberlain was a butcher in the 1870 Census.

[85] The Titmans were first mentioned in Carrie's record of "Births." He was a hotel keeper, (1880 Census).

[86] Williams could be Cora Williams, age 26, wife of Gideon (1880 Census).

[87] Minnie is 10-year-old Minnie, daughter of Hannah. This was probably a device for putting pleats in clothing.

[88] Could this be Mrs. Gordon?

[89] This could be the wife of Augustus Carpenter.

[90] In the 1880 Census there was a Charley Case, visiting with Dealys.

[91] A Charley white, 46, miner, was living with John Wood in 1880.

[92] Brother—this may be a church name for a fellow church member, as if this is Thomas Butler he is not a blood brother.

[93] Grandpa??

[94] George is the 33-year-old son of Ellen Roby? (1880 Census).

[95] Urich: Carrie had not yet learned how to spell this name, it turns out to be John Urich, miller.

[96] Thurston Roby is the brother of Varina Roby Wolf, who married August Wolf, 25 January 1880. He is 19 in the 1880 Census. They are children of Ellen Roby, widow, on the 1880 Census.

[97] Griffith Roberts, age 61, lived with Larry Ott.

[98] Thomas Aram, age 22, son of John and Sarah.

[99] Bill Anderson, miner, 47.

[100] This may be the Jake Riley mentioned later.

[101] There is no record in the Idaho County cemetery records for Charley Huston/Houston. He was obviously buried in the original burial grounds in Grangeville or at Mount Idaho. Huston's monument has been lost to time.

[102] Mrs. Robie was possibly Ellen Robie, widow, age 52.

[103] Morris Howard, 56, miner.

[104] This is Carrie's little sister, Ada Benedict.

[105] This funeral may be for Josie Crooks who died 21 April 1883 and was buried in Grangeville, whose stone was apparently moved when the great move was made from China Hill Cemetery to the newer Prairie View Cemetery in the early 1900s. Josie was born Dec. 1873 and was the daughter of J. W. and V. C. Crooks. According to Mike Peterson, this original reference is wrong. Nellie Crooks was the daughter of James and Lucy Fields Crooks. Lucy died in 1873. James and Josie Graham married in 1879. Josie, the step-mother, died 21 April 1883.

[106] Silas Reynolds? age 34, farmer.

[107] Francis is 14, daughter of William and Sarah Yates, (1880 Census).

[108] Addie and Tom Pearson are age 12 and 16, children of William and Isabella.

[109] Nellie Crooks, age 7, in 1880 Census.

[110] Probably of Alexander & Friedenrich store.

[111] Phillip Helmer, age 43, stockman.

[112] This might be Eugene Mook, a 23-year-old soldier from Camp Howard.

[113] George Hashagen; Robert Nugent, age, 32, herder.

[114] Alice is Allie Riggings, age, 13, daughter of John and Asenath.

[115] Leroy, 13-year-old brother of Oliver & A. H. Gordon.

[116] This might be Surridge. If so, James and Thomas were in the 1880 Census.

[117] Perhaps Cornelia Eccles, Divorced housemaid, age 28, in June 1880 Census. She was a sister-in-law to Mary Adkison. Her former husband, Jonathan, was "disabled," according to the 1880 Census. Cornelia's maiden name was Castle. She married Jonathan Eccles and divorced him. Later, she married James Remington of Salmon River.

[118] Mother Isabella turned 31 on November 26.

[119] Mrs. Mary D. Swarts and her daughters, Della and Birdie.

[120] Mike might be Mike Crooks who married Mary A. Behean on August 1, 1879 at the parsonage of Rev. J. D. Flenner. He was 28 and she was 17. Michael died about September 30, 1884, he is supposedly buried in Prairie View, but there is no marker and no record. Michael and Mary had two children, John M. and Katie C.

[121] Aurora Shumway, 56, farmer, divorced, (1880 Census).

[122] Possibly James Chamberlain, age 19, son of James and Angellica (1880 Census).

[123] Could be George and Hattie or James and Angelina Chamberlin.

[124] Henry Wolf, age 49, miner lived near Larry Ott.

[125] Dan Estella Bowers, age 29 and 19.

[126] Joseph Bauer, age 28, from Camp Howard.

[127] Samuel Melbourn, age 47, miner.

[128] George Rauch, age 2, and Henrietta, age 4.

[129] Probably Anton Friedenrich, age 29, general merchandise store.

[130] Forney?, James, visiting lawyer in 1880 Census.

[131] Widow, Hannah Rice and her children.

[132] If Frank Strobe, he was age 35, miner, (1880 Census).

[133] This was Christmas Day 1879—no mention of gifts, but there was mention of dancing. They fed 12 men plus their own family that day. The next day, December 26, they set about to play and have a sleigh ride.

[134] Could be George Foss, 18-year-old horse trainer.

[135] Parenthesis by Carrie—Joseph, 18, and Ed McNeir, 20, lived together.

[136] This was New Year's Eve, 1879.

[137] Probably Michael Woodward, 59, farmer.

[138] Douglas F. E. Pring, 20, grainer, (1880 Census).

[139] Mrs. John Adkison; Hattie Brown Adkison.

[140] If Walter Fenn, age 16, on 1880 Census. He did not die.

[141] They sent for the doctor on Tuesday and he arrived on Wednesday.

[142] This could be Beck or Berk.

[143] Mr. Markham was Nathaniel, age 50, or his son Frank, 23 (1880 Census).

[144] Ferdinand Hicks? Age 34, painter (1880 Census).

[145] Jaundice maybe?

[146] Ella Fairfield, 13, enumerated with Melissa Rice, her mother (1880 Census).

[147] Mrs. Bentz—Emma M. (Crooks) Bentz, married in 1876.

[148] These parentheses are from her text.

[149] Binnard. This could be Birka, 60, or Aaron, 20, both single (1880 Census).

[150] Albert W. Talkington, age 29, butcher, single (1880 Census).

[151] Fred Rice was the 8-year-old son of widow Hannah Rice.

[152] William S. Schmadeka, age 19, son of George & Sophia Schmadeka.

[153] Mary Holohan, age 18, sister-in-law of Alex McKinley (1880 Census).

[154] James Welch, age 22, cousin of Alex McKinley (1880 Census).

[155] This is the first of Carrie's reports for the mumps, which continues for several weeks as it spread through their acquaintances.

[156] Carrie herself was the second person she reported with mumps.

[157] Mr. Webber—there were four Webbers: John, 52, Louis, 19, Mat, 30, Albert, 23.

[158] The third one with mumps in 15 days.

[159] New Note. Darr has been credited with starting the myth of the cross tattoo on Pat Brice.

[160] "buy som" was crossed out.

[161] Westly Little, age 27, farmer (1880 Census).

[162] George Otterson, 26, farmer (1880 Census).

[163] Most likely Rover was a dog.

[164] Probably Mrs. Rauch.

[165] Ben Morris, farmer, age 36, from Denver, Idaho.

[166] Grant is the fourth reported with mumps since February 5.

[167] Mr. Chapman could be A.D. Chapman, age 40, stock raiser, or Israel Chapman, age 50, farmer.

[168] Ad Chapman. Arthur "AD" Chapman had gone to be a translator for Howard after his ill-conceived shot began the hostilities at White Bird. At the suggestion of Colonel Miles, Chapman went with the Nez Perce to Fort Keogh, then Fort Leavenworth, and then Indian Territory. He was now again in Idaho. See McDermott, *Forlorn Hope*, p. 161.

[169] Addie is the fifth report of mumps since February 5.

[170] The baby was the sixth one to be reported with mumps in one month and one day.

[171] William Rainey, assessor, age 38, with Lena A. Bowers.

6

AFTER 1879
Late Life, Children, and Descendants

Edward Robie

Edward Robie was born in New York on 10 February 1833, the son of John Robie and Sarah Ladd Robie.[1] His family arrived on the Mayflower and he was an eighth generation American. Some family members claim his father fought in the American Revolution, although it began 56 years before Edward's birth. Edward was, apparently, trained as a miller early in life. As a young man Edward began to drift west and was in Paris, Illinois, when the Civil War broke out. At St. Louis, Missouri, on 5 August 1861, Edward was assigned to Company B of Bissell's Missouri Engineer Regiment of the West. In five months, he was a sergeant and soon after a lieutenant.

The engineers built canals for gunboats, cleared debris from the Mississippi and repaired railroad lines. He was in Vicksburg, Mississippi, in July1863 when Confederate General John C. Pemberton surrendered and the Mississippi was opened for the Union. Next, Robie's regiment went to Nashville to repair rails and build a road to the Tennessee River. On 27 June 1864, near Johnsonville, Tennessee, he suffered sunstroke and spent three weeks in the hospital. Robie returned to duty as his regiment went to Georgia. Near Atlanta, he had sunstroke again and spent fifteen days in the hospital. He returned to join General Sherman on his famous march to the sea. Robie was in Savannah, Georgia, on 22 December 1864, when it surrendered.

In April of 1865, Robie was in Washington, D. C. for the grand review at the end of the war. He was mustered out on 22 July 1865 at Louisville, Kentucky.

After discharge, he lived at Mazeppa, Minnesota for a while. Letters indicate he was there by July of 1868. Soon he migrated to Idaho at the Slate Creek area, mining in summer, and spending the winter of 1872-73 at Idaho City in the Boise Basin.

In the winter of 1874-75, he moved a bit down the Salmon River and established himself at White Bird village. According to the family history, the next spring he packed his blankets on his back and headed to the "mining region," one hundred miles away. Half of his journey required snowshoes. This was somewhere near the Florence region, apparently, which is a lot less than one hundred miles.

Robie had partners there and they employed six or seven Chinese at $50 per month plus room and board. They made several strikes of high-quality gold and netted up to $17 per ounce, thus clearing their mine of debt.

On January 28, 1877, Edward wrote from Kamiah, Idaho, to his niece, Miss Adda M. Brown in Georgetown, Madison County, New York, explaining his circumstances.

Figure 6.1 The Robie ranch house on the River of No Return. This may be the 1890 photo taken by Hanson. Photo from the collection of Deborah Starr.

"You want to know where I am living and if there is any one else living there. Well, there are plenty of people here such as they are. Five white men, three women and four children all told, and three or four hundred Indians, how is that? I am one of the government employees on the Nez Perce Reserve. The Agency is at Lapwai. Kamiah is a sub-agency about 50 miles above on the Clear Water river. We have a church, schoolhouse, Gristmill, Saw mill, Carpenter shop, Black Smith shop, and a farm. Our school Teacher and farmer are married men and have their families here. The Rev. Mr. Fee is teacher and his wife is matron. They have two girls here. There were three but one of them went to Oregon last fall to attend school. Mr. Redfield is farmer. He has a wife and two little boys. Then we have a lady teacher, Miss McBeth. She has a school by herself and teaches theology. Peter Stegg is engineer, an old sailor and a German. Mr. G. W. Sharp is blacksmith, is a discharged soldier and hailes from New Jersey. As for myself I run the Gristmill, Sawmill, and Carpenter Shop and make myself generally useful for a thousand dollars a year. Now you know all of us. We are all good people and have to walk the Scratch while we are here and set an example for the Indians to follow.

We have preaching three times every Sunday. Mr. Fee preaches in the morning and some of the Indians in the afternoon and evening. Five of Miss McBeth's scholars are studying for the Ministry but none of them have been ordained yet. They preach in the Nez Perce Language. I go to hear them sometimes. I can tell what they say but I don't know what they mean. I only know a few words of the language but I like to hear them sing which they all do old and young. The house is always crowded and you would laugh to see the congregation. Some sitting on the seats and some on the floor and I expect they like the floor the best, and the Papooses tied onto boards standing up around the crowd."

Figure 6.2 Isabella with Emily, Edward V. and Alice. I suspect this was taken after the death of husband Edward and son George William. This would be approximately late 1889. Hanson had a studio in Grangeville which is where the picture was taken. Photo from the collection of Deborah Starr.

After the war, Robie, in partnership with Peter Smith, paid $850 for the mining claims of war-victim and old family friend James Baker. This area was on the Salmon River four miles north of Slate Creek at the area later known as Russell Bar.[2] This became the Robie home.

The new Edward W. Robie household was in Grangeville on the 1880 Census, which was taken just a couple of months after his marriage to Isabella. Edward was listed as 42, born in New York, and a miner. Wife Isabella (Kelly Benedict) was 31 years old. All four Benedict children were at home with them. Soon the family moved to his ranch on the Salmon River between Slate Creek and White Bird Creek.

On 6 September 1880, Emma "Emily" Ruth Robie was born at White Bird. In 1882, Edward Victor Robie was born at White Bird. About 1884, George "William" Robie was born. January 3, 1888, the last child, Alice Robie, arrived to join the family. According to Robie's obituary: He raised Isabella's four children as though they were his own. He ranched, and with partner, Peter Smith, expanded his cattle and mining operations. He also served as a school trustee and a county commissioner.

In the fall of 1880, Isabella persuaded son Grant to go back to school.[3] He attended the Old Columbia River Conference Academy when the Rev. W. A. Hall was in charge. Later, Grant apprenticed as a carpenter and worked at that trade for many years.

In early September 1884, Isabella's former brother-in-law died.

Leander "Lee" Dougherty, Sister Sarah's husband, was "found on a sandbar in the Payette River a mile above Miner's bridge at Horseshoe Bend. The body was considerably decayed. The remains were

Figure 6.3 Warren, Idaho in 1880. Mary Caroline taught here. Her term was 3-4 months for $80 per season. In 1880 she would have been 14, so I suspect it was some time after that that she was the teacher. Photo from the collection of Deborah Starr.

In the U. S. Court of Claims.

December Term, 189*0*.

No.*3496* INDIAN DEPREDATION CASES.

*John Bower - Administrator of the estate of
John J. Manuel, deceased*

vs.

THE UNITED STATES, AND

The Nez Perces INDIANS.

PETITION.

To the Honorable Court of Claims of the United States:

The petition of *John Bower, Administrator of the estate of John J Manuel deceased* respectfully represent that *he is a resident of Idaho County, in the State of Idaho. and that the said John J Manuel was native born, and was all his life a* citizen of the United States.

Your petitioner further states that *the said John J. Manuel* was the sole owner of the following described property, of the value as herein stated, which was, without just cause or provocation, taken or destroyed by the _____ *Nez Perces* Indians, on or about the *14th* day of *June* 18*77*, in *Idaho* County, in the State of *Idaho (then Territory)*, and not returned or paid for, to wit:

Figure 6.4 *The claim that John Manuel's estate filed for compensation. Isabella's would have used the same format.*

taken to Placerville where the funeral took place on Tuesday. The last seen of Dougherty was at Jerusalem about two weeks ago. He had delirium tremens. His clothes were found on a bank at Jerusalem.[4]"

In 1887, Grant Benedict and T. M. Pearson completed a wagon road to White Bird Creek from Grangeville.[5] This was a difficult undertaking going down the steep hill his mother had once climbed in terror with his two sisters.

In May of 1888, J. J. Manuel filed a claim for Indian Depredations with the United States Court of Claims. This court had been set up to hear and pay claims resulting from the Indian wars. They were to make recommendations to Congress and Congress would then have the ultimate financial decision. Hundreds of claims had been filed, but the court claimed the proofs were weak. Isabella and many others in the area also filed claims at this time.

On 6 October 1888, Isabella's brother-in-law, Alexander Orchard, Mary Ann's husband, died at Idaho City.[6] The local newspaper, *The Idaho World*, wrote a major story about his life. He had suffered from severe rheumatism for 20 years, and lately had developed dropsy. He stayed cheerful despite his problems and told his physician, Dr. Zipf,

Figure 6.5 Domecq ranch, down stream and adjacent to the Robie ranch on Salmon River. Photo from the collection of Deborah Starr.

that he had no fear of death. He was buried with Masonic ritual. He left wife, Mary Ann, and five sons.

In 1888, the Robie ranch on The River of No Return had many head of cattle, many various fruit trees, and Edward was still mining some of the time. He was also elected a school trustee, and in November was elected a County Commissioner. He had to travel to Mount Idaho for those meetings.

On a stormy day, 20 February 1889, Edward Robie left home to attend a horse sale two miles down river on Skookum Creek at the home of Mr. Bouffard. Apparently in good health, Robie had a heart attack and was found dead on the trail by Tony Gordon who was returning from the sale. Coroner Bibby conducted an inquest. Widowed for the second time, Isabella had seven children at home to feed, and Grant was earning his own living.

Isabella filed for a government pension claiming Robie's ill health resulted from his Civil War service. "She used affidavits from his

Figure 6.6 Jeanette's daughter Maggie Manuel as a youth and in her elder years. Photo from the collection of Deborah Starr.

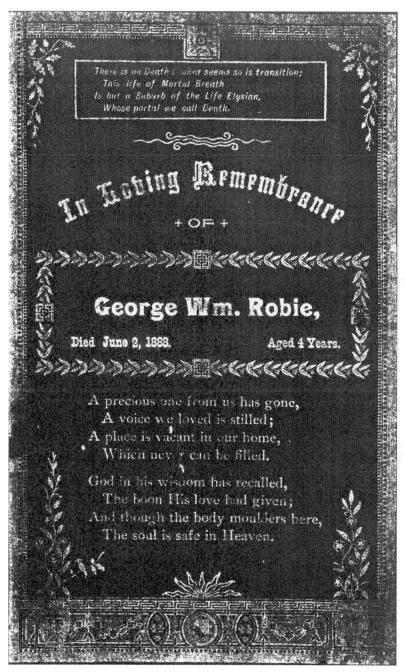

Figure 6.7 Funeral memento from the death of George William Robie, June 1889. Photocopy from the collection of Deborah Starr.

commanding officer and a letter from Peter Smith to convince the War Department that he had never recovered."[7] She was granted $12 a month from the war department which she drew until 1911. Tragedy struck again that year with the death of George William Robie, Isabella's 4-year-old son on June 2, 1889.[8] Smallpox was the cause of death. The year 1899 was a terrible one for Isabella.

Isabella continued with her claim for losses suffered in the Nez Perce conflict.[9] In May of 1890, 13 years after the start of the war, Indian Agent, Orlando "Rube" Robbins, who was J.D. Williams' sidekick in supervising the New Year's Ball of 1863, and in the shoot out with Cherokee Bob that followed, came to Camas Prairie and Salmon River areas. He called together Nez Perce tribal members to get their testimony about events of the war.[10] A newspaper report from Boise read:

"On May 22nd, Indian Agent Robbins expects to call together all members of Chief Joseph's band for the purpose of getting proofs concerning the depredations made during the Nez Perce War (1877). Hundreds of depredation claims have been sent from the department to Mr. Robbins for inquiry into the facts. All parties who have claims against the government arising from injury received or service rendered during the Nez Perce war, can if they wish, be present either by person or by attorney, and assist in the adjustment of their claims. These claims will, when acted upon, be forwarded at once to the Commissioner of Claims in the department at Washington.[11]"

Isabella listed all the buildings and the other items lost.[12] She said she had never returned to their old home in all these years. She lived quite close, at the Robie ranch, but not close enough to relive those days. She surely must have remembered Robbins, the man who worked the dance floor partnered with her friend, Jeanette's soon-to-be first husband.

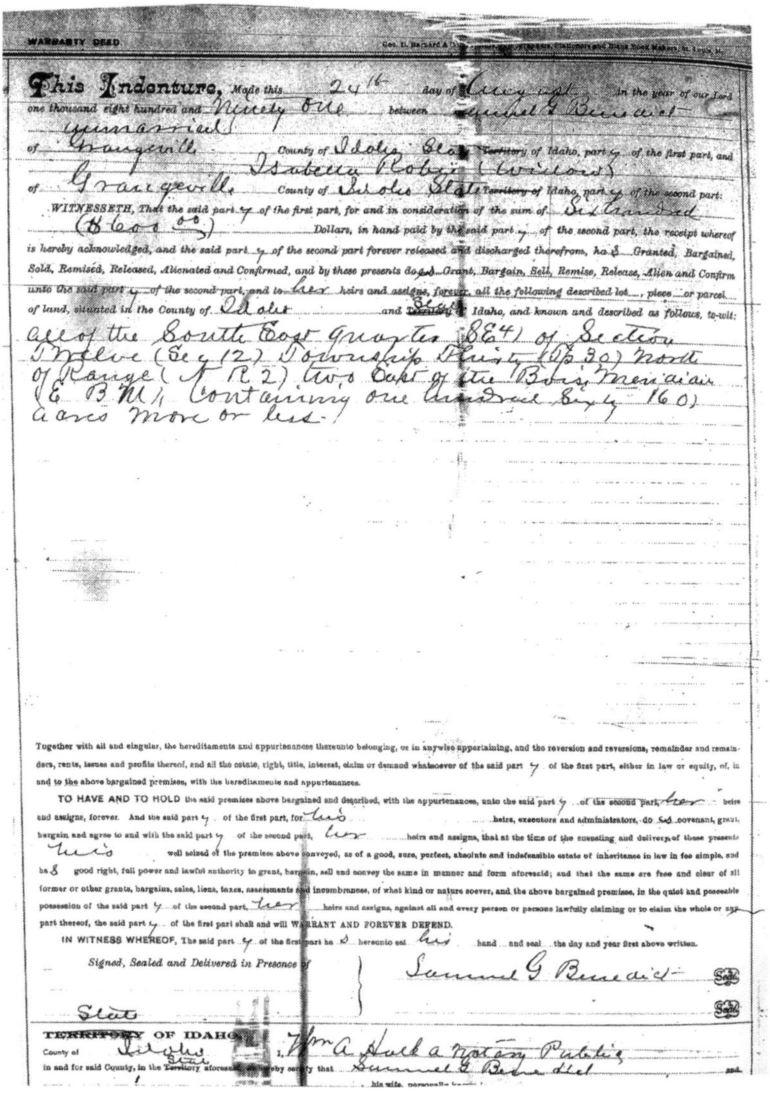
WARRANTY DEED

This Indenture, Made this 24th day of August in the year of our Lord one thousand eight hundred and Ninety One between Samuel G Benedict (unmarried) of Grangeville County of Idaho State of Idaho, part y of the first part, and Isabella Robie (widow) of Grangeville County of Idaho State of Idaho, part y of the second part:

WITNESSETH, That the said part y of the first part, for and in consideration of the sum of Six Hundred ($600.00) Dollars, in hand paid by the said part y of the second part, the receipt whereof is hereby acknowledged, and the said part y of the second part forever released and discharged therefrom, ha s Granted, Bargained, Sold, Remised, Released, Aliened and Confirmed, and by these presents do es Grant, Bargain, Sell, Remise, Release, Alien and Confirm unto the said part y of the second part, and to her heirs and assigns, forever, all the following described lot..., piece ... or parcel of land, situated in the County of Idaho and State of Idaho, and known and described as follows, to-wit:

all of the South East Quarter (SE¼) of Section Twelve (Sec 12) Township Thirty (Tp 30) North of Range (N R 2) two East of the Boise Meridian (E B M) Containing one Hundred Sixty (160) acres more or less.

Together with all and singular, the hereditaments and appurtenances thereunto belonging, or in anywise appertaining, and the reversion and reversions, remainder and remainders, rents, issues and profits thereof, and all the estate, right, title, interest, claim or demand whatsoever of the said part y of the first part, either in law or equity, of, in and to the above bargained premises, with the hereditaments and appurtenances.

TO HAVE AND TO HOLD the said premises above bargained and described, with the appurtenances, unto the said part y of the second part, her heirs and assigns, forever. And the said part y of the first part, for his heirs, executors and administrators, do es covenant, grant, bargain and agree to and with the said part y of the second part, her heirs and assigns, that at the time of the ensealing and delivery of these presents his well seized of the premises above conveyed, as of a good, sure, perfect, absolute and indefeasible estate of inheritance in law in fee simple, and ha s good right, full power and lawful authority to grant, bargain, sell and convey the same in manner and form aforesaid; and that the same are free and clear of all former or other grants, bargains, sales, liens, taxes, assessments and incumbrances, of what kind or nature soever, and the above bargained premises, in the quiet and peaceable possession of the said part y of the second part, her heirs and assigns, against all and every person or persons lawfully claiming or to claim the whole or any part thereof, the said part y of the first part shall and will WARRANT AND FOREVER DEFEND.

IN WITNESS WHEREOF, The said part y of the first part ha s hereunto set his hand and seal the day and year first above written.

Signed, Sealed and Delivered in Presence of

Samuel G Benedict [Seal]

[Seal]

State OF IDAHO,
County of Idaho

I, Wm A Hall a Notary Public in and for said County, in the State aforesaid, do hereby certify that Samuel G Benedict and his wife, personally ...

Figure 6.8 Deed when Isabella sold land to her son Grant Benedict.

During the warm, light months of 1890, the photographers Hanson and Erichson, or least one of them, came around the Robie ranch and the Salmon River area to photograph the Nez Perce War sites. For Isabella, this must have painfully brought to mind events she did not wish to relive.

In August of 1891, Isabella sold her son, Grant, a quarter section of land (160 acres) for $600.[13]

Frances Benedict married Harry F. Shissler of Grangeville on 6 December 1891.[14] He was born in Warren, Idaho, 18 October 1868, the son of Mr. and Mrs. Franklin Shissler. Harry was destined to add several colorful chapters to the family history.

On September 25, 1892, Mr. Brown married Addie Benedict at Grangeville.[15] The two rescued children of 1877 were now married women.

Jeanette Manuel, who disappeared permanently the night before the White Bird Battle while Isabella was hiding along the trail, was never forgotten and many events led to new re-livings of her old tale. For instance, in 1895 a human skeleton was found near the mouth of White Bird Creek. Local people speculated that this, at last, was Jeanette Manuel's previously un-recovered body.[16] Grant Benedict, son of Isabella and her war-victim first husband, said the remains had a large skull and the frame was that of a massive man. He believed it was that of the Umatilla Indian his father had killed in 1876, a year before the war.[17] Whoever it was, it did not appear to have been the remains of the petite Jeanette.

In 1896, L P. Brown, founder of Mount Idaho died. Nineteen years before this, his leadership and largess had saved many settlers at his hotel in that village.[18] In October of 1896, Isabella's daughter, Mary C. (Caddie or Carrie) Benedict Wilson, who had written the diary during her rooming house days, sued her husband John Wilson for divorce at Grangeville.[19]

Harry F. Shissler

In 1899, Isabella's son-in-law, Harry Shissler, with co-owners Nate Pettibone, John M. Shissler and Franklin Shissler, sold 200 acres of placer ground to Young and Turner for $10,000.[20] The first $1,000 was in cash as the company added to its 18 claims in that rich gold district.

When the great Thunder Mountain gold rush struck Idaho, Harry was quick to see an opportunity. H. O. Stechhan arrived in

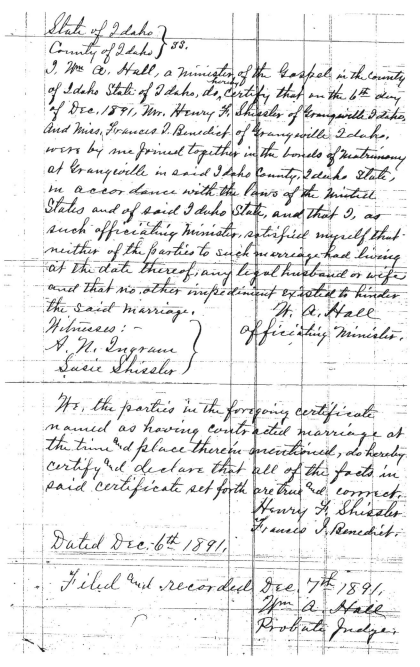

State of Idaho }
County of Idaho } ss.

I, Wm A. Hall, a minister of the Gospel in the county of Idaho State of Idaho, do hereby Certify that on the 6th day of Dec. 1891, Mr. Henry F. Shissler of Grangeville Idaho, And Miss. Frances I. Benedict of Grangeville Idaho, were by me joined together in the bonds of matrimony at Grangeville in said Idaho County, Idaho State, in accordance with the laws of the United States and of said Idaho State, and that I, as such officiating minister, satisfied myself that neither of the parties to such marriage had living at the date thereof, any legal husband or wife and that no other impediment existed to hinder the said marriage.

Witnesses: —
A. N. Ingram
Susie Shissler

W. A. Hall
Officiating Minister.

We, the parties in the foregoing certificate named as having contracted marriage at the time and place therein mentioned, do hereby certify and declare that all of the facts in said certificate set forth are true and correct.

Henry F. Shissler
Frances I. Benedict.

Dated Dec. 6th 1891.

Filed and recorded Dec. 7th 1891.
Wm A Hall
Probate Judge.

Figure 6.9 Marriage record of Frances Benedict to Henry Shissler, 6 December 1891.
Photocopy from the collection of Deborah Starr.

Boise from Thunder Mountain in June of 1902 with a tale involving Shissler. "Now I'm going to tell you something that is a matter of common rumor, but I will not vouch for its absolute truthfulness, for I do not know. It is the story that M. L. Murray of Elk City and Harry Shissler of Newsome Creek have jumped the Sunnyside claims, and are prepared to defend themselves against all comers. They allege that they have discovered some flaws in the locations. As these claims were sold to the Belle of Thunder Mountain Company for $125,000, if rumor should prove to be true it will cause all kinds of trouble."[21]

Before long, Harry Shissler had additional personal trouble that had to greatly influence Isabella's later years.[22] Shissler was running a saloon at Stites, Idaho, near Kooskia at the confluence of two forks of the Clearwater River. Shissler went to the restaurant that blacksmith E. W. Williams ran in partnership with Mrs. Minnie Harris. She was said to have a husband in Montana and he had a wife and six children in Washington State. Shissler went to talk to Mrs. Harris about her life style. An alternate explanation said Shissler was interested in a young woman that worked there and he came into the place drunk. Mrs. Harris berated him and ordered him out. He challenged her, "If you have any son of a bitch that can put me out, bring him on."[23]

When Williams returned home he heard about the exchange and found Shissler who returned to the restaurant with him. In response to Williams' question, Shissler admitted to his earlier visit and the remarks he had made. Williams told him not to do that again and shoved or hit Shissler. Shissler drew his 44 caliber and struck Williams and immediately fired a shot at him. Williams

Figure 6.10 Tombstone of Loyal and Sarah Brown, proprietors of the Mt. Idaho Hotel in 1877.

Figure 6.11 Angelena and Herman C.
Brown at the Mt. Idaho Cemetery. Photo
by the author.

Figure 6.12 Tombstone for John and
Jeanette Manuel at Mt. Idaho Cemetery.
Photo by the author.

Figure 6.13 George Popham [Jeanette
Manuel's father] tombstone, beside the
Manuel marker at Mt. Idaho Cemetery.
Photo by the author.

drew his revolver and fired. Witnesses had a difficult time recalling the details that ensued, but when the fight was over, Williams gun had three empty chambers and Shissler's had four empty. One bullet went into Williams' abdomen and lodged in his spine, killing him.

Shissler turned his gun over to authorities and an inquest was held before Williams was cold. Shissler, who was out on bonds from Federal Court on a charge of bootlegging on the reservation, was charged with murder. Shissler was shot twice in the exchange with Williams, once between the bones of his forearm and once in the side.

The Odd Fellows Lodge at Stites assisted in getting Edward W. William's body sent to Garfield, Washington for burial.[24]

The trial was at Grangeville, with witness Hattie Haight giving the most damning testimony. After 22 hours of deliberation, the jury reached a decision contrary to the predictions of most of the local folk. Harry was guilty of manslaughter. This would seem the conclusion of the sorry event, but it was just a beginning.

Harry Shissler Goes Free

**CUTS HIS WAY OUT OF JAIL, WITH TOOLS SMUG-
GLED IN TO HIM, AND NOW HAS THE WHOLE WIDE
WORLD BEFORE HIM**[25]

Harry Shissler is no longer a prisoner of Idaho County.

He got away, Wednesday night, and may have gone to Boise to serve his term in the penitentiary, but perhaps he didn't.

Word was received Monday that a company of friends were on the way here to ask for Mr. Shissler's release. The sheriff fixed up a little reception for them, with hot coffee and other things on the side—principally other things. The friends, however did not appear. A large guard was kept over the jail that night, and the next, but no one appeared.

Wednesday night was as dark as the darkest dungeon that ever chilled the heart of a prisoner. Two guards were patrolling about the jail, while the jailor and Deputy Sheriff Blackburn were in the jail. It is the custom of the jailor to put the prisoners out of the main corridor, into their cells, a little after 8 o'clock. That night, when he went to lock up, at 8 o'clock, Shissler was gone. He had in some way secured a brace and bit, bored a hole through the floor of the corridor, and got out by crawling through the water and mud around to the point in the jail where he made his exit. But he was gone, to a certainty, and so far no search has been successful in finding him.

Shissler's wife had visited him earlier in the evening, just before supper.

Sheriff Greene, who started Sunday for St. Anthony with George Dennison for the state reform school, was called back by the news of the alleged jail delivery, and reached here Monday night. He made sure it was a false alarm, and then started again with his charge to St. Anthony. He would be somewhere over in Oregon, presumably, at the time of the escape.

There is no doubt that the escape could and should have been prevented. The outside guards were expected to see any such movement. The dark night, however, made it impossible to see more than a few feet.

After the rumored rescue, Monday night, Jailor Berry made a thorough search of the place, but failed to find any tools or other suspicious indications. The escape was made by boring holes through the floor, close enough to make a continuous cut, and removing a section of the floor about two feet square. It is indicative of the construction of the jail, that in making the complete circuit of the hole, close to eight feet in all, that he did not once strike a nail. The floor, like the rest of the jail, is constructed of planks laid together, and presumably nailed so closely as to make a network of iron all the way around. If one could make a continuous cut of 80 inches without striking a nail, it may be wondered that there was ever a prisoner left for trial.

It is understood that the sheriff left orders for Shissler to be confined in the steel cell, but that he begged off, claiming to have a serious bowel trouble, making it necessary for him to have free access to the water closet, where he made his escape.

An advertisement in the Standard would be certain to reach the missing man, but its doubtful if he would come back.

As time passed Shissler began to become almost legendary. "One man claimed to have met him in the mountains, where he had been metamorphosed into an almond eyed chink with a long flowing pigtail and a broque that would put a phonograph to route."[26] One man swore he had drunk heavily with him out in the open until the wee hours. Shissler was seen everywhere. As one local newspaper opined,

*Figure 6.14 Cartwright Family. Isabella's sister and brother-in-law.
Photo from the collection of Deborah Starr.*

"he is a sort of an Ancient Mariner, a Wandering Jew, a disembodied spirit, a willo' the wisp, a man hard to catch, and pretty slippery when you do catch him."[27]

The tales were satisfying, but not true. Shissler had indeed escaped from the County jail. He passed within a few feet of the sheriff's deputies and heard the instructions they received to shoot him onsight. He went down from Camas Pairie toward Stites and even talked with the men who were guarding the road there in anticipation of his expected route of escape. Shissler was unarmed that night, and at one point heard the buggy full of sheriff's men approach in the dark. Shissler laid down in the road and was mistaken for a lage pile of mud when his presence freightened their horses.

Shissler went down the Clearwater River by way of Culdesac, skirted around Lewiston and crossed the Snake River on the ferry near Asotin. Then into California, and finally into Goldfield, Nevada. At Goldfield, he met

Figure 6.15 Christie Orchard Davis, Isabella's niece. Photo from the collection of Deborah Starr.

people from Idaho County and feared he would be turned in. He returned to Idaho County until October when he traveled south once again.

He went overland to Pomeroy, Washington, and then straight to Salt Lake City. There he got sick and was bedridden for about two weeks. Then he went to Reno where he was re-captured. While traveling around California, Nevada and Utah, Shissler took the name of Billy Smith, grew a moustache, and worked as a professional gambler. Other gamblers called him "Smithy."

At Reno, an unnamed person recognized him, and told the police. Chief-of-Police R. C. Leeper of Reno, with a deputy, went to make the arrest. They approached Shissler, ordered him to stand, and slapped the cuffs on. When they momentarily relaxed he went for his gun. They put a gun to his head and he surrendered peacefully. He was taken to Boise and put in the penitentiary. He spoke of a new trial and hoped he wouldn't have to spend all eight years of his sentence there. He also said he had $500 the last time he left Idaho County, but lost it all gambling.

In mid-November of 1906, Idaho County's Sheriff Green was in Boise getting extradition papers to bring Shissler back to Idaho.[28]

Sheriff Green of Idaho County gave Chief Leeper a $250 reward for the capture. In December of

Figure 6.16 Christie Orchard Davis, Isabella's niece. Photo from the collection of Deborah Starr.

1908, attorney James Fogg of Lewiston petitioned the Idaho Board of Pardons to release Shissler. Family story says he served three years. His request for a pardon was "continued" by the pardon board in 1909.[29] By 1910, he was released, and the Shisslers were both living in Newsome, Idaho. They then moved to Montana to avoid embarassment.

Harry died in Carter, Montana on 5 July 1923.[30] He was brought back to Grangeville for burial. W. N. Knox, a former schoolmate of Harry officiated at the funeral. Knox was also the widowed husband of Julia Manuel Bowman, thus Jeanette Manuel's son-in-law. The connections between the ladies' families never ended.

Isabella's Daily Life

In September 1905, Mr. M. R. Thompson, a purchasing right-of-way agent for the North Pacific Railroad, and Dr. M. F. Kenneley of Grangeville, left for the Salmon River to consult with Isabella about land she sold the city for a terminal grounds.[31] There was a "legal hitch" in the deed, but they thought they could clear it up.

On August 22, 1908, Edward V. Robie married Mamie A. Large at Grangeville. They lived at Slate Creek and ranched.

Kelly Family Renunion

In 1911, the three daughters (Isabella Robie, Sarah Cartwright and Mary Ann Orchard) of Mr. and Mrs. John Kelly, held a reunion in Boise.[32] In their 40 years in Idaho, they had never all been together. They told their life stories for the newspaper reporter. All three were born in New York, went to California with their parents during the gold rush, and then lived in Oregon, in the Willamette Valley. Isabella, Sarah and their father went to Idaho in 1861, but Mary Ann did not immediately join them. Father Kelley operated a store in Florence and Isabella worked with him.

Mary went to Boise Basin later, about 1864, when their father, John, moved there to pursue a career in politics, and her sisters had married. The other Kelly sisters led mundane lives compared to Isabella. Isabella was the sister with the dangerously exciting and tragic life story to share that reunion day in Boise.

The reunion article told again the story of Isabella's involvement in the war but added a few unique details. Mr. Benedict was shot in both legs, according to this story, but escaped temporarily inside his house. That evening he was called out and shot 18 times by the Indians. The hired man, Mr. Bacon, shot an Indian, but then the Nez Perce killed him too. Mrs. Benedict and "her little babe" (she only has one child with her in this version) were taken captive but the "squaws took pity on the white woman and after a few days succeeded in arranging her escape." Later, while crawling through the brush, a band of Indians came by just as the baby started to cry. The braves stopped at once but one of the Nez Perce women, realizing what the sound was, shook her own child and admonished it. The Indians went on. "Mrs. Robie kept until death the baby shoe in which she scooped up the water for herself, and child to drink during the period of escape." Isabella was described in 1911 as wonderfully preserved, and bright, and able to read without glasses.

Isabella's Death

This reunion was none too soon. On the following June 6th, Isabella Kelly Benedict Robie was stricken with a stroke of paralysis, and died four days later (June 10, 1911) surrounded by all her children and her two sisters.[33] She was remembered at that time as a pioneer and victim of the Nez Perce War. She was survived by six children: Mrs.

W. G. Brown, Grangeville; Grant Benedict, Grangeville; Mrs. Frank (Frances) Shissler, Elk City; Mrs. Frank M. Taylor and Mrs. Pitt (Pickett) Chamberlain, White Bird; and Miss Alice Robie, Boise.[34] She was buried at White Bird Cemetery between White Bird village and Slate Creek village. On Monday, June 12, the Reverend Father James of Grangeville conducted the service. Her tombstone said Isabella Robie/1847-1911/Requiescat in Pace. There is a cross on the stone and on the top edge the word mother. Nearby are the tombstones of Edward V. Robie, 1882-1920; and Mamie A. Robie

Figure 6.17 Isabella's tombstone in Whitebird Cemetery. She rests between the sites of the Benedict store and the Robie ranch. Photo by the author.

1885-1967. Isabella was a remarkable Idaho pioneer. Her perseverance, work ethic, bravery, and commitment to family made her life story a quintessential part of Idaho's early history. She was mother to a whole clan of descendants who contributed greatly to the State of Idaho. Bless you, pioneer mother from the River of No Return.

J. J. Kelly Returns to Idaho, 1916

In 1916, Isabella's youngest sibling, John James Kelly of Staten Island, New York, visited Idaho for the first time in 47 years.[35] He claimed a remarkable memory, and that seemed to be true in regards to places and buildings. He did, however, have a few erroneous memories in his story in the *Statesman* of Boise. He said, for instance, Isabella married Robie at Florence and that she died at Walla Walla. While in the Idaho area, he visited his grandniece, Marie Davis, and his aunt, Mrs. Cartwright in southern Idaho.

Mrs. Sarah Cartwright, wife of George Cartwright, died at the family home on Schafer Creek of pneumonia following influenza at the beginning of 1919. Her obituary related that Mrs. Cartwright was 65 years of age, coming to the Basin in 1865 with her parents, Mr. and Mrs. John Kelly. Before her marriage, she lived at Granite Creek. She was survived by her husband and two sons, Arthur and Calvin, and a sister, Mrs. Mary Orchard of Boise. The two young men are convalescing from influenza. Mr. Cartwright having to assume entire care of the other three sick persons, owing to the difficulty in getting outside help. No funeral arrangements have been made.[36]

Mary Ann Orchard

On 9 February 1927, Mary Orchard died at the home of her daughter, Mrs. R. K. Davis, in Boise.[37] She had lived there for 25 years. She left her sons: W. L. Orchard, Jess Orchard of San Francisco, H. A. Orchard, and Mrs.

MRS. GEORGE CARTWRIGHT, a Pioneer of '64, Who Died Recently.

BOISE BASIN PIONEER SEES THRILLING TIMES WHEN WEST WAS WILD

Mrs. George Cartwright Came to Idaho in 1861 and Witnessed Growth of Idaho.

Known and beloved by all the pioneers of the Basin and many of Boise was Mrs. George Cartwright, who was one of the victims of influenza, passing away at her home at the Cartwright ranch on Shafer creek last month.

Mrs. Cartwright was born in Tompkinsville, L. I., and was 65 years of age. When but a child she moved with her family to California, making the trip from New York by water on the old ship "Sierra Nevada," the time consuming 21 days. Later the family located at Portland, Ore., and came to Idaho in 1864.

Mrs. Cartwright often told of the tedious ride from Umatilla to the Basin, which she made with her family on a saddle train, and of many other interesting experiences and hardships of the early days.

She leaves her husband and two sons, Arthur and Calvin, and a sister, Mrs. Mary Orchard, who resides with her daughter, Mrs. R. K. Davis, of Boise, and also a brother, John J. Kelly, of New York. The greatest sorrow of Mrs. Cartwright's life was the loss of her only daughter, who died a number of years ago at the age of 16 while attending school in Weiser.

Figure 6.18 Sarah Kelly Dougherty Cartwright obituary clipping.

Davis, her only daughter. She had eight grandchildren, four great grandchildren and one brother, John J. Kelly of New York, according to obituaries that were published several places in the state.

The Children of Isabella

Isabella's life was over, but the lives of her children were an extension of hers. The generations go on endlessly, but the lives of her children will complete her life story here.

Emily Robie

Emily married Picket Chamberlin. They had a son and two daughters and she died in 1939.

Edward Victor Robie

Edward married Mamie Large and they had a big family. In 1920, Ed Robie was killed when he was thrown from a horse and dragged. Mamie continued to operate the ranch, and died at age 81.

Alice Robie

Alice married Ralph Russell on 14 October 1914 at White Bird, where he operated a ranch. They had two sons. He died in 1950, and she died in 1972 at the Latah Convalescent Center in Moscow, Idaho.

Grant Benedict

When his brother-in-law Billy Brown, became sheriff, Grant began a 30-year-career as a jailer at the court house. Nearing the age of 80, he was attacked and beaten in the face with a hammer by a desperate prisoner. He never recovered and spent the last eight years of his life in Seattle living with his son. He died on 9 December 1951. He was buried in Cavalry Cemetery. Mrs. Carrie Perkins Benedict, born in De Soto, Iowa, on 17 March 1879, died on November 1938. She married Grant on 24 June 1895. She was buried at Prairie View Cemetery as a Christian Scientist.

Frances Isabella Benedict Shissler

Harry and Frances Shissler moved to Great Falls, Montana, when he was released from prison. He died in 1923, and she moved to Bonners Ferry, Idaho, to live with her sister. Frances and sister, Addie, bought the Grignon Place in Paradise Valley and were still there in 1939. Frances Died on September 23, 1955 at Marysville, Washington. She had lived with Addie for 35 years.[38]

Adelaide "Addie" Benedict Brown

Mr. William Green Brown, Addie's husband, was the marshal of Grangeville and later the sheriff of Idaho County. He died 30 December 1945 at Spokane. She died on 22 December 1964 at Marysville, Washington. They had five children.

Elizabeth Castello Wood

Mrs. Elizabeth Castello Wood died December 10, 1936, at her home in Monterey, California. Her obituaries disagreed on her marriage date as 1866 or 1869. She was the mother of nine children. After years living at Slate Creek, she had moved to Seattle and then California in the final few years of her life. She was born 20 December, 1851 on Staten Island. Her obituaries did not adequately explain her relationship with the Kelly family.

The Robie Brothers, Grandsons

According to Bob Painter, Bill, Peck and Ralph Robie put on "Slate Creek Rodeos" in 1938 and 1939 at the Ben Large place north of Slate Creek along highway 95. These were the sons of Edward V. Robie.

By 1964, the children of Isabella had all passed away. The first stage of Isabella's legacy was over, but her future descendants continue without end.

Figure 6.19 Edward V. Robie tombstone, Whitebird Cemetery. This was Isabella's son who died in a horse accident in 1920, after his mother's death. Photo by the author.

Figure 6.20 Photo of George Popham late in life. His obituary had the most erroneous information of any character in this book. Photo from the collection of Deborah Starr.

Figure 6. 21 Portrait of Edward V. Robie. Photo from the collection of Deborah Starr.

Figure 6.22 Ed Robie and others on horseback. Fred Lyda, Ed Robie, Pick Chamberlin, Frank Taylor. Taken at Fred Lyda homestead on Slipper Creek, Idaho. Photo from the collection of Deborah Starr.

Figure 6. 24 Grant Benedict with Friend. Photo from the collection of Deborah Starr.

Figure 6.23 Grant Benedict with son and Grandson. Photo from the collection of Deborah Starr.

Figure 6.27 Addie Benedict as young girl. Photo from the collection of Deborah Starr.

Figure 6.26 Maggie Manuel Bowman in later life. Photo from the collection of Deborah Starr.

Figure 6.25 Grant Benedict in later life. Photo from the collection of Deborah Starr.

Figure 6.28 Mary Caroline Benedict with baby Lester Taylor. Photo from the collection of Deborah Starr.

Figure 6.30 Henry Shissler and Frances I. Benedict, Grangeville, Idaho 1896. Photo from collection of Mike Peterson.

Figure 6.29 Frances Benedict Shissler, Pat Taylor and baby Deborah Taylor (Starr). Photo from the collection of Deborah Starr.

End Notes

[1] Two secondary sources that give a biographical sketch of Robie are: Kathy Deinhardt Hill, *Spirits of the Salmon River*. Cambridge, Idaho: Backeddy Books, 2001, pp. 172-176, and Zona Chedsey and Carolyn Frei, eds. *Idaho County Voices: A People's History from the Pioneers to the Present.* Idaho County Centennial Committee, 1990, pp. 260-261. Some sources list his birth as 20 June 1834.

[2] Kathy Deinhardt Hill, *Spirits of the Salmon River*. Cambridge, Idaho: Backeddy Books, 2001, pp. 172-176.

[3] Adkison, J. Loyal. "Benedict Family Closely Related to Early Idaho History," *Idaho County Free Press*, 27 March 1952.

[4] *Idaho World*, Idaho City, 5 September 1884.

[5] *Idaho County Free Press*, Grangeville, Idaho, 11 March 1887.

[6] *Idaho World*, Idaho City, 9 October 1888, p. 1, c. 3-4.

[7] Kathy Deinhardt Hill, *Spirits of the Salmon River*. Cambridge, Idaho: Backeddy Books, 2001, pp. 172-176.

[8] This date is on the program from the funeral. Some sources say that he died before his father.

[9] This was claim no. 10557, signed 9 November 1889. See McDermott, *Forlorn Hope*, p. 10.

[10] *Idaho Daily Statesman*, 21 May 1890, p. 1, c. 6.

[11] *Idaho Daily Statesman*, 21 May 1890, p. 1, c. 6. Quote from the *Lewiston Teller*.

[12] The list of buildings, fruit trees and livestock may be found in Chapter Three of this book. Other items enumerated include: two beds, and bedding, consisting of mattresses, quilts and pillows. 12 cane bottom chairs, rugs, six cheap paintings, one feather bed, seven patchwork quilts, eight pair blankets, eight or 10 pillows, and enough clothing for the whole family to last three years. There was also a library of assorted books, a gold watch, 2 purses of gold dust, a gold watch and chain, one black enamel breast pin, two sets of gold sleeve buttons, one set of earrings, two gold crosses, one single barrel shot gun, and one five shot Smith and Wesson revolver.

[13] Idaho County Deed Book 8, p. 204.

[14] Copy of document in author's possession.

[15] *History of North Idaho*, 1903, p. 530. Biography of William G. Brown.

[16] Helmer, *Warren Times, A Collection of News About Warren, Idaho*. Wolfe City, Texas: Hennington Publishing Co., 1988. No page number.

[17] *Idaho County Free Press*, Grangeville, Idaho, 9 September 1965.

[18] *Genesee News*, Genesee, Idaho, 17 April 1896, p. 1, c. 5.

[19] Copy of District Court Document in author's possession.

[20] *Idaho Daily Statesman*, 14 November 1899, p. 4.

[21] *Idaho Daily Statesman*, 24 June 1902, p. 6, c. 1.

[22] This whole story in shortened form is found at http://idaho.idgenweb.org/murders/wms_shissler_murder,htm. Accessed 29 January 2012. This source is based on clippings from the *Idaho Daily Statesman* of Boise, 13 September 1905, 4 April 1906, 27 November 1906.

[23] *The Standard*, Grangeville, Idaho, 23 June 1905, p. 1, c. 1-2.

[24] *The Grangeville News*, Grangeville, Idaho, 24 June 1905.

[25] *The Standard*, Grangeville, Idaho, 27 Oct. 1905, p. 1, c. 1-2. This is quoted in its entirety so as not to dilute the local flavor.

[26] *The Standard*, Grangeville, Idaho, 6 March 1906. p. 1, c. 5.

[27] *The Standard*, Grangeville, Idaho, 6 March 1906. p. 1, c. 5.

[28] *Idaho Daily Statesman*, 11 November 1906, p. 6, c. 1.

[29] *Idaho Daily Statesman*, 8 July 1909, p. 6, c. 1.

[30] *Idaho County Free Press*, Grangeville, Idaho, 11 July 1923. Shissler ranched several years in Montana, and then operated a hotel in Carter the last three years of his life. He was survived by his aged mother, Elizabeth S. Shissler, sister Mrs. N. B. Pettibone, brothers J. M. of Grangeville, and George S. of Elk City.

[31] *Grangeville News*, Grangeville, Idaho, 5 September 1905, p. 8, c. 3.

[32] *Idaho Daily Statesman*, Boise, Idaho, 23 July 1911, p. 3, c. 1-4.

[33] *Idaho County Free Press*, Grangeville, Idaho, 15 June 1911.

[34] *Idaho Daily Statesman*, 13 June 1911, p. 10, c. 2.

[35] "Visits Boise for First Time in 47 Years; Remembers How Old Fort Looked," *Idaho Statesman,* 8 Oct 1916. *Idaho Daily Statesman*, 13 June 1911, p. 10.

[36] *Idaho Statesman*, 4 January, 1919, p. 5, c. 4.

[37] *Idaho Statesman*, 10 February 1927, p. 7, c. 7.

[38] J. Loyal Adkison, "Survivor Nez Perce Indian War Dead, Marysville, Wash.," *Idaho County Free Press*, Grangeville, Id, 1955.

Appendix

Family Trees for Isabella
Her Husbands and Their Children

A. Family of Nurture of Isabella Kelly (Benedict Robie)

Father

John M. Kelly

> B. 6 November 1820. Ireland
>
> D. 18 October 1868, Granite Creek, Idaho

Mother

Sarah O'Donnell, B. 1817? (1820?) Ireland

Children

Isabella Kelly

> B. 26 November 1848. Richmond, Staten Island, New York
>
> M. Samuel Benedict, 7 February 1863, Florence, Idaho
>
> Five children together
>
> M. Edward W. Robie, 19 April 1880
>
> Four children together
>
> D. 15 June 1911, Slate Creek, Idaho

Francis Kelly

> B. 1849, New York

Mary Ann, Kelly
> B. 28 March 1852, Tompkinsville, NY,
> M. Alex Orchard, B. 1836 D. 6 October 1888.
> 7 children together.
> D. 9 Feb. 1927, Boise, Idaho

Sarah Kelly
> B. 6 July 1853, Tompkinsville, NY
> M. Leander Dougherty, 7 Jan 1868 at Boise
> Lee Dougherty, husband, died Sept 1884
> M. George Cartwright
> D. 1 January 1919, Shafer Creek, Idaho

James John (John James) Kelly,
> B. 1860, Portland, Oregon

Elizabeth Green Castello (foster daughter)
> B. 20 December 1851, Staten Island, New York
> M. Wood
> 9 children
> D. 10 December1936, Monterey, California

B. Samuel Benedict, Family of Nurture
Father
Smith Benedict
> B. ca 1800, Died 9 April 1889

Mother
Dorcus "Tricky" Cole, B. 18 May 1813,
> D. October 1888

Children
Samuel
> B. 20 August 1835. The oldest of 11 children, plus there were
> two half-siblings from his father's first marriage.
> D. June 1877, Whitebird, Idaho

C. Samuel Benedict and Isabella Kelly Family
Father
Samuel Benedict
> B. 20 August 1835, D. June 1877

Mother
Isabella Kelly
> B. 26 November 1848, D. 15 June 1911

Children
Ulysses Samuel Grant,
> B. 9 October 1864, Freedom, Idaho
> M. Carrie Perkins, 17 (19?) June 1894, Grangeville, Idaho
> D. 9 December 1951

Mary Caroline, B. 10 September 1866, Lewiston, Idaho
> M. John Wilson, 1888
> Divorced. October 1896
> M. Frank Lester Taylor, 22 December 1896
> Seven children together.
> D. 25 December 1916

Frances Isabella
> B. 9 October 1868, Whitebird, Idaho
> M. Henry Shissler, 6 December 1891
> D. 23 September 1955

Nettie
> B. 1871
> D. Sept. 1873, Whitebird, Idaho

Adelaide
> B. 4 November 1873
> M. William Green Brown, 30 September 1892
> D. 30 December 1945

D. Edward Robie, Family of Nurture

Father

John Robie

Mother

Sarah Ladd Robie

Children

Edward Robie
> B. 10 February 1833
> M. Isabella Kelly Benedict, 19 April 1880. Grangeville, Idaho
> D. 20 February 1889, Whitebird, Idaho

E. Edward Robie and Isabella Kelly Benedict

Father

Edward Robie
> B. 10 Feb. 1833
> D. 20 February 1889

Mother

Isabella Kelly
> B. 26 November 1848
> D. 15 June 1911

Children

Edward Victor Robie
> B. 25 March 1882
> M. Mamie Agnes Large, 22 August 1908, Grangeville, Idaho
> One daughter and two sons
> D. May, 1920, Whitebird, Idaho

George "William"
> B. ca 1884
> D. 2 June 1888, Whitebird, Idaho

Sarah "Alice"
>B. 3 Jan 1888
>M. Ralph James Russell, 14 October 1914, Whitebird, Idaho
>Two sons together
>D. 16 January 1972, Moscow, Idaho

Emma "Emily" Ruth B. 16 Sep 1880
>M. Pickett Chamberlin, 6 June 1906
>Two daughters and a son
>D. 6 Sept 1939, Lewiston, Idaho

BIBLIOGRAPHIC ESSAY

THE SOURCES for some parts of Isabella's story are numerous, but for other parts sparse indeed. Observers, reporters, historians and human memory fail to agree on how or when things happened. There are many sources about the 1863 New Year's dance and the gunfight that resulted from it. None give much mention to Isabella's presence. Her involvement in the start of the Nez Perce War and the events around the Battle of White Bird are also well documented, but sources disagree on details and many observers were more interested in defending their own actions than explaining the events. The family members kept newspaper clippings over the years, and filled out questionnaires regarding family history. These are valuable resources, despite the limits of the details of citation.

My own work on John and Jeanette Manuel, (*Jeanette Manuel, The Life and Legend of the Belle of Fabulous Florence.* Heritage Witness Reflections Publishing, Troy, Idaho, 2009) has as much about the two great events in Isabella's life as any work available. But her life was more than those two great events.

Isabella wrote several letters and gave several reminiscences of the events that are very helpful. The Lewiston *Teller* of 26 April 1878 (p. 1, c. 4-5) has a letter from Isabella explaining her memories of the incident in 1875 when Samuel killed a Nez Perce man. Daughter Frances (Mrs. Shissler) told her memories in detail in 1939 (*Bonners Ferry Herald*, Bonners Ferry, Idaho. 6 April 1939, p. 1, c.1 & 2, p. 6,

c. 2 & 3.). This has been reprinted in numerous sources and posted on the internet. Grant recorded his version of some of the events, although he was in Mount Idaho, not on White Bird Creek at the time. Many people, peripherally involved, left reminiscences as well. Helen Walsh wrote a long letter to the Lewiston newspaper two months after the events. See *The Teller*, Lewiston, Idaho, 8 September 1877, p. 2, c. 1-3.

The Battle at White Bird and the events around that time were covered by J. D. Flenner in the *Idaho Sunday Statesman*, 8 October 1911, Section II, p. 1-7, plus. Jack Wilkins' article in the *Lewiston Tribune* on 9 July 1957 was based mostly on Frances Shissler's memoir. The best coverage of the events leading to the battle and the whole start of the war remains with John McDermott's. *Forlorn Hope*. Boise: Idaho Historical Society, 1978.

In 1920, Major Frank Fenn wrote "Frontier Justice" in which he told of Benedict's involvement with the Fat Jack debacle in Florence. Fenn was a long-time resident who was personally involved in many of the events told in his tales. The *Florence Miner* of 8 January 1898 tells probably the best version of the New Year's dance and subsequent gun fight. The town of Florence boomed a second time in the 1890s and a newspaper was started there. The microfilmed copies of this paper are nearly impossible to read, but worth the effort. The article is a reprint of an article from a Lewiston newspaper, but I have been unable to find the original. Some early Lewiston newspapers are no longer extant.

Mary Caroline's diary was kept in the possession of Evan Mark Taylor at Lewiston for many years. The transcription was originally typed and edited by Carol Anglen, who was active in the genealogy society on the Camas Prairie. I owe a great debt to the hard work she did on the diary project.

The *Lewiston Tribune* of 24 July 1977, 100 years after the events, had a story about the war. They used material from Alice Russell, gathered 20 years before, and other standard sources.

J. Loyal Adkison and Norman B. Adkison wrote extensively over a period of years in books and newspaper articles about these events and people. As local residents they had an understanding of the people and geography involved that is extremely valuable. Another local resident, Charlotte M. Kirkwood, (*The Nez Perce War Under War Chiefs Joseph and White Bird*) used information gathered and synthesized over years to write her version of events.

In 9 September 1965, the *Idaho County Free Press* of Grangeville reprinted tales of the finding of a skeleton in 1895 at Horseshoe Bend. The Nez Perce War itself has a large and ever-growing body of interpretive work done by many historians. Some of these histories are good while others seem driven by the author's overall interpretation, and lack any attempt at analytical scholarship.

Annotated Bibliography

(Anonymous) A Practical Miner. [Metlar, George W.] *Northern California, Scott & Klamath Rivers, Their Inhabitants and Characteristics—Its Historical Features—Arrival of Scott and His Friends—Mining Interests. A True Portrait of the Miner, His Habits and Customs or Attributes of Character—Estimation of the Nice Young Man by the Ladies—Our Climate and Geographical Features—England's Vain Glorious Boasting—American Nationality Contrasted—Historical Incident Connected With General Washington, Together With a Life-Like Picture of San Francisco.* Yreka, CA: Yreka Union Office, 1856. This history describes the movement to the Salmon River mines and the various individuals who later came to Idaho.

Adkison, J. Loyal. "Benedict Family Closely Related to Early Idaho History," *Idaho County Free Press*, 27 March 1952. Adkison wrote a biographical sketch of Grant Benedict upon his death.

Adkison, Norman B. *Indian Braves and Battles with More Nez Perce Lore.* Grangeville, Idaho: *Idaho County Free Press*, 1967. As a local man, Adkison could well relate the opinions of local people about the Nez Perce War.

Adkison, Norman B. *Nez Perce Indian War and Original Stories.* Grangeville, Idaho: *Idaho County Free Press*, 1966. Local stories of the Nez Perce War.

Adkison, J. Loyal. "Survivor Nez Perce War Dead Marysville, Wash," *Idaho County Free Press*, 1955, p. 1, c. 1-3. On the death of Frances Benedict, Adkison again wrote his version of the war events.

Ancestry.com: Full Context of *Idaho County Free Press*, Vital Records, 1886-1903. An excellent source for vital statistics from Idaho County.

Bailey, Robert G. *River of No Return*. Lewiston, Idaho: R. G. Bailey Printing Comp., 1983. Bailey discussed many of these events with individuals who had been there years before, and judged the amount of accuracy the stories retained.

Baird, Dennis, Mallickan, Diane, and Swagerty, W. R. *The Nez Perce Nation Divided*. Moscow: University of Idaho Press, 2002. An excellent source for documents and discussions of their meaning in the early settlement in Idaho.

Bancroft, Hubert Howe. *The Works of Hubert Howe Bancroft, History of Washington,*

Idaho, Montana, 1845-1899, Vol. 31. San Francisco: The History Company, 1890. A contemporary source on Idaho early events.

Banditti of the Rocky Mountains and Vigilance Committee in Idaho, An Authentic Read of Startling Adventures in the gold mines of Idaho, 1865. A justification for the vigilante action against Henry Plummer and his alleged gang.

Boessenecker, John. *Gold Dust and Gunsmoke: Tales of Gold Rush Outlaws, Gunfighters, Lawman, and Vigilantes*. New York: John Wiley & Sons, 1999. This gives much of the early history of Cherokee Bob.

Boone, Lalia. *Idaho Place Names: A Geographical Dictionary*. Moscow: University of Idaho Press, 1988. This is a basic source to locate and identify Idaho places.

Brown, Alonzo F. "The Autobiography of Alonzo F. Brown," *Echoes of the Past*, Vol. 1, no. 2, August 2002, pp. 8-15. part II in Vol. 1, no. 3, February 2003, pp. 14-22. This material by Brown can also be found in several other places. It is a basic source on life in Florence during the gold rush.

Brown, Mark H. *The Flight of the Nez Perce*. New York: G. P. Putnam's Sons, 1967. An introduction to this sad conflict.

Carrey, Johnny, and Conley, Cort. *River of No Return*. Cambridge, Idaho: Backeddy Books, 1977. This book covers the geography and history of the Salmon River.

Casey, Penny Bennett. Transcription of "Marriage Book in the Idaho County Courthouse." http://www.rootsweb.com/-idaho/marriages.htm. An excellent source for vital records in the Idaho County region.

Converse, George L. *A Military History of the Columbia Valley, 1848-1865*. Walla Walla, Washington: Pioneer Press Books, 1988. This tells of the soldiers who went to the White Bird Battle and the handling of their remains.

Dakis, Mike and Dakis, Ruth. "Guilty or Not guilty? Vigilantes on Trial," *Idaho Yesterdays*, Winter 1968-1969, pp. 2-5. A counter-balance to the evaluations of the vigilantes they wrote themselves.

Defenbach, Byron. *Idaho the Place and Its People, A History of the Gem State from Prehistoric to Present Days.* 3 Volumes. Chicago: American Historical Society, 1933. A basic history of Idaho, covering many of the events in the present book.

Dempsey, Hugh. "The Tragedy of White Bird: An Indian's Death in Exile," *Echoes of the Past*, Vol. 1, no. 8 September 2005, pp. 10-17. The story of the Nez Perce leader who was closely associated with the area around the Village of White Bird.

Denny (Byington), Jenny. Interview with author, 7 May 1998. Jenny is a direct descendant of Jeanette Manuel and owns many of the artifacts from the Manuel family.

DeVeny, Betty. "Slate Creek History," Typescript, March 1974. This gives many sources and facts on the beginning of this town.

Dimsdale, Thomas J. *The Vigilantes of Montana*, Norman, 1953. A vigilante interprets the value and necessity of the vigilante movement.

Elliot, Wallace W. *History of Idaho, The Territory: Showing Its Resources and Advantages.* San Francisco: Wallace W. Elliot, 1884.

Elsensohn, Sister M. Alfreda, *Pioneer Days in Idaho County* . 2 Volumes. Caldwell, Idaho: Caxton Printers, 1947, 1951. Sister Alfred gathered and published histories of the area and began a museum which remains at the Monastery of St. Gertrude.

"Fabulous Florence," *Idaho Yesterdays*, Summer 1962, pp. 22-31. A brief description of the town's early, violent history.

Fisher, Don, "Nez Perce War," Masters Thesis, University of Idaho, 1925. A research project that included an interview with Maggie Manuel Bowman.

A General Directory and Business Guide of the Principal Towns East of the Cascade Mountains for the Year 1865. San Francisco: A. Roman & Co., 1865. This primary document tells of many businesses and business owners during the early days.

Gibbs, Rafe. *Beckoning the Bold The Story of the Dawning of Idaho.* Moscow: University of Idaho Press, 1976. A history of Idaho with emphasis on the exciting parts.

Gibson, Elizabeth. "The Fate of Cherokee Bob," http://www.suite101.com/article. cfm.349/15757. An internet source using secondary sources.

Gulick, Bill. *Outlaws of the Pacific Northwest.* Caldwell, Idaho: Caxton Press, 2000. A noted writer covers some of the old ground again.

Haberman, Mike. "Vanishing Florence: An Early Idaho Mining Metropolis Disappears Into History," *Lewiston Morning Tribune,* 2 August 1998, Sec. D. p. 1. This article described the new interpretive kiosk at Florence.

Hailey, John. *The History of Idaho.* Boise, Idaho.: Syms-York Company, 1910. A history of Idaho by a man who knew many of the people covered.

Hampton, Bruce. *Children of Grace: The Nez Perce War of 1877.* New York: Avon Books, 1994. A readily available book on the War.

Hart, Arthur A. *Basin of Gold: Life in Boise Basin, 1862-1890.* Idaho City: Idaho City Historical Foundation, 1986. A popular history of the Boise Basin region.

Hart, Arthur, "To Serve and Protect, a History of the Boise Police Department, 1863-2000. This book mentions Orlando "Rube" Robbins time as a police chief.

Hawley, James H. *History of Idaho, The Gem of the Mountains.* 3 Volumes. Chicago: S. J. Clarke Publishing Co., 1920. Another basic Idaho history written by a man who knew many of the people of the era.

Hegne, Barbara. *Virginia City: Rascals & Renegades Plus a Few Forgotten People of the Comstock Lode.* Sparks, Nevada: published by the author, 2000.

Helmers, Cheryl. *Warren Times, A Collection of News About Warren, Idaho.* Wolfe City, Texas: Henington Publishing Co., 1988. Helmers collected information on Warren from newspaper accounts in regional newspapers.

Hendricks, George D. *The Bad Man of the West.* Revised Edition, San Antonio, Texas: The Naylor Company, 1959. A brief discussion of Cherokee Bob is included in this book.

Hill, Kathy Deinhardt. *Spirits of the Salmon River.* Cambridge, Idaho: Backeddy Books, 2001. The historical characters and their burial sites are discussed.

History of Siskiyou County, California, Illustrated with Views of Residences, Business Buildings and Natural Scenery, and Containing Portraits and Biographies of Its Leading Citizens and Pioneers. Oakland, CA: D. J. Stewart & Co., 1881. The Pophams, Jack Manuel, J. D. Williams, and others lived here before moving to Idaho.

Howard, Helen Addison. "Did Chief Joseph Slay Mrs. Manuel?" *Frontier Times,* January 1972, p. 22-48. An account in a popular magazine by an actual historian.

Howard, Helen Addison. *War Chief Joseph: Saga of Chief Joseph.* Lincoln: University of Nebraska Press, 1978. Howard's longer study of the war.

Howard, O. O. *Nez Perce Joseph: An Account of his Ancestors, His Lands, His Confederates, His Enemies, His Murders, His War, His Pursuit and Capture.* Boston: Lee and Shepard Publishers, 1881. Howard was the commanding general during the war but was not at all places at all times and had his own viewpoint.

Hunter, George. *Reminiscences of an Old Timer: A Recital of the Actual Events, Incidents, Trials, Hardships, Vicissitudes, Adventures, Perils, and Escapes of a Pioneer, Hunter, Miner, and Scout of the Pacific Northwest, Together with his Later Experiences in Official and Business Capacities . . . The Several Indian Wars, Anecdotes, etc.* Battle Creek, Michigan: Review and Herald, 1889.

Hussey, Larry. *Fort Walla Walla, Then and Now*. Walla Walla, Washington: Privately printed, 1994. This was the fort that supplied soldiers to Lapwai and to the war.

Idaho State Historical Society, Sixteenth Biennial Report. 1938. Some of the correspondence between Governor Brayman and Orlando Robbins was printed in this issue.

An Illustrated History of North Idaho. Western Historical Publishing Company, 1903. The story of the beginning of the war seems based on Maggie Manuel's memory. "Impressions of the Boise Basin in 1863," *Idaho Yesterdays*, 1863, p. 8. Basin Basin gold was discovered shortly after Florence's.

Jones, J. Roy. *Saddle Bags in Siskiyou*. c. 1953, Reprinted Happy Camp, CA: Naturegraph Publishers, 1980. More history of the Californians who later went to Idaho.

Kirkwood, Charlotte M. *The Nez Perce War Under War Chiefs Joseph and White Bird*. Grangeville, Idaho: Idaho County Free Press, n.d. (195?) This local author knew the principals for years and gathered significant insights.

Langford, Nathaniel Pitt. *Vigilante Days and Ways: The Pioneers of the Rockies; The Makers and Making of Montana, Idaho, Oregon, Washington and Wyoming*. Missoula, Montana: University Press, 1957. (Reprint of 1890 book.) Langford was a vigilante himself, and created dialogue, but his work must be considered in the effort to find the truth and consider all points of view.

Lewis, William S. "Spent Boyhood Days at Old Fort Colville," *Spokesman Review*, Spokane, Washington. This describes the background of Duncan McDonald who wrote about the Nez Perce who escaped to Canada.

Limbaugh, Ronald Hadley. "Attitudes of the Population of Idaho Toward Law and Order, 1860-1870," Masters Thesis, University of Idaho, 1962. This covers early bad men in Idaho in a professional manner.

Limbaugh, Ronald Hadley. "The Idaho Spoilesmen: Federal Administrators and Idaho Territorial Politics, 1863-1890," Ph.D. dissertation, University of Idaho, History Department, 1966. Further study on Idaho legal system.

Lindstrom, Joyce, ed. *Idaho's Vigilantes*. Moscow: University of Idaho Press, 1984. This is a compilation of work written about vigilantism in Idaho.

Lyman, W.D. *Lyman's History of Old Walla Walla County Embracing Walla Walla, Columbia, Garfield and Asotin Counties*. 2 Volumes. Chicago: S. J. Clarke Publishing Co., 1918. This work covers some of the individuals and events associated with the Nez Perce War.

Mather, R. E. and Boswell, F. E. *Gold Camp Desperadoes: A Study of Violence, Crime, and Punishment on the Mining Frontier*. San Jose, California: History West, 1990. A new look at the vigilante issues that does not accept their word for their rationale.

Mather, R. E. and Boswell, F. E. *Hanging the Sheriff*, Internet http://www.yanoun. org/mony-vigi/hangnew/calif3.html. Discusses Henry Plummer in particular, and questions his guilt.

Mather, R. E. and Boswell, F. E. *Hanging the Sheriff: A Biography of Henry Plummer*. Salt Lake City: University of Utah Press, 1987. Same as the internet source on Plummer.

McBride, John R. "Idaho Pioneer Reminiscences," Microfilm no. 45. U of Idaho Library. McBride was an Idaho judge who saw many of these events from his unique perspective.

McConnell, William J. *Frontier Law, A story of Vigilante Days*. In collaboration with Howard R. Driggs, New York: World Book Company, 1926. McConnell lived in the Payette Valley when he was doing his vigilante work but he was aware of others in other areas.

McDermott, John. *Forlorn Hope*. Boise: Idaho Historical Society, 1978. An excellent book on the events at the start of the Nez Perce War.

McDonald, Duncan. "Goaded to the War-Path," *The New Northwest* (Deer Lodge, Montana), 21 June 1878. McDonald had relatives among the people he interviewed.

McKay, Kathryn L. *Gold for the Taking: Historical Overview of the Florence Mining District, Idaho County, Idaho*. United States Department of Agriculture, Nez Perce National Forest, Grangeville, Idaho, 1998. A good study of the early history of this now-deserted area.

McWhorter, L.V. *Hear Me My Chiefs: Nez Perce History and Legend*. Caldwell, Idaho: Caxton Printers, 1986. The natives had an opportunity to explain their side of the events.

McWhorter, Lucullus Virgil. *Yellow Wolf: His Own Story*. Caldwell, Idaho: Caxton Press, 2000. Yellow Wolf was involved in the war and knew many of the principals.

Mills, Nellie Ireton. *All Along the River: Territorial and Pioneer Days on the Payette*. Montreal: Payette Radio Limited, 1963. This book mentions Mary Ann Kelly Cartwright's home.

Nez Perce, Summer 1877. Nez Perce National Historical Park, Montana Historical Society Press, 2000. Another history of the War.

"Nez Perce War Letters to Idaho Governor Brayman," *Fifteenth Biennial Report of the Board of Trustees of the Historical Society of Idaho for the Years 1935-1936*. The war letters help to understand the flow of the events.

Olson, William, Collection, Special Collections, University of Idaho Library. Olson spent years on basic research and turned up many rare documents.

Oros, Walter M. "In Commemoration of John Hailey and Orlando Robbins," *Nineteenth Biennial Report of the Idaho State Historical Society, 1943-1944*. Boise, Idaho. Tells a bit about Robbins involvement in various events.

Owsley, Barney. Reminiscences. typescript. (The story of a Pioneer, 90 years old, whose earliest experience associate him with practically all the famous men of early territorial days.) J. A. Harrington Collection. Oboler Library, Idaho State University, Pocatello, Idaho. (1937). Owsley was quite young while in Florence and quite old when he recalled his version of event.

Pacific Coast Business Directory for 1867. San Francisco: Henry G. Langley, 1867. The businesses in these towns are listedPainter, Bob. *Tales of the Breaks: True Stories from Along the "breaks" of the Snake, Salmon and Clearwater Rivers*. n.p: second revision, 2007. Painter lived in the area and study these events over a long period.

Painter, Bob, *White Bird: The Last Great Warrior Chief of the Nez Perces*. Fairfield, Washington: Ye Galleon Press, 2002.

Peltier, Jerome. "The Brief Inglorious Life of Cherokee Bob," *The Spokesman Review*, 10 February 1957. An account based mostly on Langford's work.

Reinhart, Herman Francis. *The Golden Frontier: The Recollections of Herman Francis Reinhart, 1851-1869*. Austin: University of Texas Press, 1962. Reinhardt traveled to all the early Idaho mining camps and remembered things well.

Roberts, R. M. *Scout,* New York: Ballentine Books, 1956. Paperback novel. Based on Orlando "Rube" Robbins in the Bannock War of 1878.

Ronnenberg, Herman. *Beer and Brewing in the Inland Northwest, 1850-1950*. Moscow: University of Idaho Press, 1993. Covers the brewing history of Idaho, including J. J. Manuel, brewery owner in Warren.

Ronnenberg, Herman Wiley. "Cherokee Bob's Grave: The Historical and Literary Legacy From Fabulous Florence." *Echoes of the Past* (From the Historical Museum at St. Gertrude), Vol. 1, Number 6. September 2004, pp. 5-15. This work attempt to cover all that is known of the life of Henry J. Talbot.

Ronnenberg, Herman Wiley. "Gottfried Gamble," *The Golden Age* (Nez Perce County Historical Society) Vol. 27, no. 1, spring and summer, 2007, pp. 21-24. Included because it covers the mine that J. J. Manuel invested in.

Ronnenberg, Herman Wiley. *Jeanette Manuel, The Life and Legend of the Belle of Fabulous Florence*. Heritage Witness Reflections Publishing, Troy, Idaho, 2009. This is the only biography of Isabella's closest friend.

Ronnenberg, Herman Wiley. "John J. Manuel, Idaho Mining Camp Brewer and Nez Perce War Victim," *American Breweriana Journal,* No. 164, March-April, 2010, pp. 20-31. A synopsis of the material on Manuel.

Ronnenberg, Herman Wiley. "Isabella Kelly Benedict Robie," *Echoes of the Past*, October, 2009, pp. 14-25. A very brief introduction to Isabella's life.

Ronnenberg, Herman Wiley. "Who Was Red-Headed Cynthia?" *The Mountain Light: The Newsletter of the Idaho State Historical Society*, Vol. 45, no. 2, Spring 2006, pp. 21-22. Cynth was Cherokee Bob's friend and previously, her last name was not even available in print.

Ronnenberg, Herman Wiley. "Raymund Saux: Idaho's French Connection," *Echoes of the Past*, Vol. 1, No. 8, March 2006, pp. 5-11. Saux bought the Warren brewery after Manuel moved to Whitebird Creek.

Ronnenberg, Herman Wiley. "Raymund Saux: Idaho's French Connection," *Echoes of the Past*, Vol. 1, No. 8, March, 2006, pp. 5-11. Same information on Saux.

Secrest, William B. *California Desperadoes: Stories of Early California Outlaws in Their Own Words*. Clovis, California: Word Dancer Press, 2000. A source for the early life of Cherokee Bob.

Shinn, M. W. "Cherokee Bob, the Original Jack Hamlin," *The Overland Monthly*, Vol. xvi, no. 91, July 1890. The first article to make a legend of the outlaw gambler.

Shissler, Frances I. (Benedict) "A Story of an Indian Uprising," *Echoes of the Past*, Vol. I, no. 1, pp. 12- 18. This is the same as the original newspaper article.

Shissler, Frances I. (Benedict). *Bonners Ferry Herald*, Bonners Ferry, Idaho, 6 April 1939, p. 1, c.1 & 2, p. 6, c. 2 & 3. Her memories of 1877.

Swanson, Chamelin, and Territe. *Criminal Investigation,* 4th Edition. New York: Random House, 1988. The book explains the condition of bodies in fires.

Talkington, H. L. "Plummer—in Vigilante Days," *Lewiston Morning Tribune*, 19 August 1917. Shows the state of the research and the current beliefs at this date.

Territory of Washington, County of Walla Walla. W. M. Ewing, Plaintiff vs. Cinthia [sic] Ann Ewing, Deft. In the District Court, first Judicial District. Photocopy in the records of William Olson, University of Idaho Library, Special Collections. This is Red—Headed Cynthia's divorce record.

Thompson & West, *History of Yuba County California*, 1879, Chapter xxxix, n.p. Covers the area where the Kelly family briefly lived.

"Vivid Recollections of Chief Joseph at Whitebird Given," *Walla Walla Union-Bulletin*, Walla Walla, Washington, 23 January 1944. The last of the many interviews Maggie gave about the start of the War during her long life.

"Visits Boise for First Time in 47 Years; Remembers How Old Fort Looked," *Idaho Statesman*, 8 Oct 1916. John Kelly, younger brother of Isabella returned to Idaho.

Walsh, Helen, letter. *The Teller*, Lewiston, Idaho, 8 September 1877, p. 2, c. 1-3. She described the killing of her brother and others at the start of the war.

Wells, Edward Lansing. "Notes on the Winter of 1861-1862 in the Pacific Northwest," *Northwest Science*, Vol. xxi, pp. 76-83. Explains the remarkably severe weather in the winter of 1861-62 when Florence was first settled.

Wilfong, Cheryl. *Following the Nez Perce Trail: A Guide to the Nee-Me-Poo National Historical Trail with Eyewitness Accounts.* Eugene: Oregon State University Press, 1990. Describes the trail and uses the 1903 history of Idaho as a source for the events at the start of the war.

Newspapers

Boise News, Bannock (Idaho City), Idaho, 1863.

The Capital Chronicle, Boise, Idaho, 1869. 1870.

Daily Alta California, San Francisco, California, 1855. 1863.

East Washingtonian, Pomeroy, Washington, 1931, 1949.

Eureka Daily Republican, Eureka, Nevada. 1877.

Evening Bulletin, San Francisco, California, 1856.

The Evening Capital News, Boise, Idaho, 1911.

The Florence Miner, Florence, Idaho, 8 January 1898.

Genesee News, Genesee, Idaho, 1895. 1896.

The Grangeville Globe, Grangeville, Idaho, 1913.

Idaho County Free Press, Grangeville, Idaho. 1887, 1889, 1890, 1910, 1961, 1965.

Idaho Daily Statesman, [aka Idaho *Tri-Weekly Statesman*] Boise, Idaho. 1875, 1887, 1888, 1905, 1909, 1911,

Idaho Democrat. Boise, 1895.

Idaho Signal. Lewiston, Idaho. 1872, 1873, 1874

Idaho World. Idaho City, Idaho. 1877. 1878

Lewiston Morning Tribune, Lewiston, Idaho, 1917. 2001

Morning Oregonian, Portland, Oregon, 1863.

New Northwest. Deer Lodge, Montana, 1878.

Oregonian, Portland, Oregon, 1870.

Sacramento Daily Union, Sacramento, California, 1861.

San Francisco Daily Herald, San Francisco, California, 1855.

The Semi-Weekly Idahoan. Boise, Idaho, 1877, 1878.

Spokesman Review, Spokane, Washington, 1920.

The Teller, (aka *Lewiston Teller*) Lewiston, Idaho, 1877, 1878.

Walla Walla Union-Bulletin, Walla Walla, Washington, 1944.

The Washington Statesman, Walla Walla, Washington, 1862. 1863.

Yreka Semi-Weekly Journal (aka *Weekly Journal*) Yreka, California, 1861-1863.

Primary Sources

Docket Book, Florence, Idaho, Olsen Manuscript Collection, University of Idaho Library, Special Collections.

Idaho County Deed Books.

Idaho County marriage records.

Idaho County Recorder's record book, .

Olson Collection, No. 393 Manuscript Group, University of Idaho Library, Special Collections, Moscow, Idaho.

INDEX

Page numbers appearing in italics refer to photographs or illustrative material. The introduction to and photographs appearing in Mary Caroline's diary are indexed but the subjects and names within the diary or chapter notes are not indexed.

Made in the USA
Middletown, DE
10 October 2018